ENGAGING ADOLESCENTS

Michael Hawton is a registered psychologist with 30 years of experience. He is a listed clinical expert with the NSW Children's Court and an expert witness in the Family Court of Australia. A former teacher, Michael has spent much of his career working with parents and their children, and has been teaching family services workers and educational leaders in the area of behaviour management for over a decade. Michael has developed parent education programs that have been taught to over 100,000 parents and professionals since 2006. A father of two, Michael brings a clear and unambiguous method-based approach to ease the distress of parents experiencing difficulties with their teenagers' behaviour.

ENGAGING ADOLESCENTS

parenting tough issues

with teenagers

MICHAEL HAWTON

EXISLE
PUBLISHING

'One of the hardest parts of living with a teenager? Simply talking to them! Michael Hawton provides some practical and down-to-earth advice on how to defuse emotionally charged situations, have a meaningful conversation with a teen, and get something accomplished.'

—Dr Tom Phelan, author of *Surviving Your Adolescents*

'This book provided me with real resources to implement and use at home. No airy fairy theories but real, practical things to say, do and live by.'

—Tina, mother of four

'A very well thought-out program which provides step-by-step strategies to engage with adolescents and have difficult conversations to bring about positive change.'

—Emma, school counsellor and mother of three

'This book gives you both the practical tools and the confidence to deal with typical teenage behaviour problems; you realize that you're not alone! Michael knows his stuff and all the material is supported by well-researched information.'

—Carol, mother of two

'Schools should insist that all parents attend — in fact, everyone needs to develop the skills taught in this course. It's a must for everyone who engages with young people.'

—Paris, teacher and mother of two

First published 2017

Exisle Publishing Pty Ltd

'Moonrising', Narone Creek Road, Wollombi, NSW 2325, Australia

P.O. Box 60–490, Titirangi, Auckland 0642, New Zealand

www.exislepublishing.com

A CiP record for this book is available from the National Library of Australia.

ISBN 978-1-925335-40-8

Designed by Tracey Gibbs

Typeset in Andes Condensed and Miller Text

Printed in China

This book uses paper sourced under ISO 14001 guidelines from well-managed forests and other controlled sources.

10 9 8 7 6 5 4 3 2 1

Disclaimer

While this book is intended as a general information resource and all care has been taken in compiling the contents, neither the author nor the publisher and their distributors can be held responsible for any loss, claim or action that may arise from reliance on the information contained in this book. As each person and situation is unique, it is the responsibility of the reader to consult a qualified professional regarding their personal care.

CONTENTS

PREFACE

For 30 years I have worked with families who are trying to organize things differently at home. I have found a lot of parents who lack confidence — and that's not such a good thing. I tend to see parents who want the very best for their teenagers, but when a difficult matter comes along, they either feel they don't have the right to butt in or just hope that the problem will fix itself.

This lack of confidence isn't all that surprising. The context for raising young people has undergone some fairly big changes. In many ways, raising teenagers today is like the experiences of immigrant families when they first settle in an adopted country. These parents often report how their children know more about what's going on in the 'new country' compared to them; they pick up the language better, they know how to navigate 'the scene' and they're critical of the way their parents do things. I suspect a fair few teenagers today see their parents as being out of touch in much the same way.

It might take a village to raise a child, but nowadays the idea of anyone other than a teenager's parent intervening to stop their son or daughter being rude or behaving badly in public is frowned upon. In fact, you're almost shunned for thinking this way. While someone watching a teenager 'going off' at their parent might raise an eyebrow or two, it's less likely that an adult who is *not* the parent will say, 'Hey, hang on there. What do you think you are doing?' And, in some instances, even if the adult was to say something, they would be admonished by the very parent who is being abused. Clearly, the 'village' idea needs some revisiting!

In my experience, the current strain felt by many parents with 'out there' kids is most obvious when two ideals come into conflict (when a teenager's drive to push the boundaries clashes with their parents' wishes to look out for their best interests). The two *biggest* issues facing parents today are how to sort out what difficult behaviour really is and how to manage it. These are the two issues which parents seek help for and the main reason I have written this book. As parents of teenagers, we all have another heart walking around out there and, if they look like they're in danger, our own hearts skip a beat. That's what comes with being attached — I get that. However, loving your child doesn't mean you should tolerate just any sort of behaviour.

It's not hard to see why so many decisions about tackling difficult behaviour get put off to the never-never due to a lack of energy. I mean, how many of us want to wrangle with the spirited soul that's our teenage son or daughter after a hard day's work? How many of us want to risk that kind of flare-up? Sometimes it seems easier just to ignore it and hope it solves itself in time. If you have felt this way, you're not alone.

That said, it's a big mistake to hit the eject button too early with poorly behaved teenagers. I've seen this too often in my own country town, where many young people were cut adrift by their parents before they were ready to cope with life. Although these young people were still living at home, their parents just didn't interfere with their lives. In fact, they lived like people who were living in a motel. I realize that trying to talk to teenagers is hard and can sap anyone's energy. It's completely understandable that many parents just run out of puff. But there are solutions to these exhausting confrontations about behaviour and I will cover these in the book.

What *Engaging Adolescents* will give you

The main process I will show you is one for resolving a teenager's *unacceptable* behaviour. It's simple; only five steps. I will also show you how to be a more confident and effective parent. I know these methods work, because more than 24,000 parents have been taught them and they say they can do it. It all boils down to knowing how to manage a problem. Although the process I will show you is primarily used to manage the behaviour of teens, it can also be used for children age ten and upwards if they have the maturity to engage with the process.

In writing this guide, I want to re-boot a much-needed debate about parenting teenagers — one where the 'new black' is a reasonable expectation that you can positively affect a teenager for the better and see the results of your efforts. Instead of having 'hallway' conversations (where everyone seemingly has an escape route) you'll be able to sort through important issues to everyone's satisfaction. Not only do I hope you will solve problems specific to your family, but you'll be able to teach your teenager to become a better negotiator — something they're likely to be grateful for when they enter relationships, live with flatmates or deal with work colleagues.

You will also be more likely to handle a problem (and not put off dealing with it) if you know what to expect. By describing what might happen at each stage in a tough conversation about the problem — and what steps you need to take to handle any reactive angst or uppityness — you will go into conversations better prepared. Being better prepared means that you will be more confident. When a problem arises I will teach you how to have conversations where you will be able to calmly manage and resolve a problem at hand.

I've certainly had lots to do with families across many years — much more than many academics — and like Malcolm

Gladwell, the author of *Blink*, says, you get pretty good at doing your job after long enough. But I want to offer you some of my own personal experience as well, as I think you will gain comfort from knowing some of the mistakes I made when I was parenting two teenagers. There were times when I chastised myself during our children's teenage years, with thoughts like: 'You're a professional working in this area. Why did you just do that? The very thing you tell others *not* to do?' In the heat of the moment, we all say things that we might later regret. My disclaimer is that you should read these pages knowing that even family professionals like me do the job imperfectly.

When I was growing up there were people in my life who noticed my sometimes self-defeating behaviour and asked for more of me. As a young man, I needed this type of direction. And I needed this prompting from a number of significant people: my parents, my aunt, my uncle, my school principal, my football coach and my college lecturer all asked that little bit extra of me. They encouraged me to be more self-disciplined, to make better use of the opportunities and chances offered to me and to consider the effects of my behaviour on myself and others. I'd have to say that I had a lot of people in my life who did not lack the gumption and the courage to tell me how it was, when I needed their guidance. If there is one theme that you will hear throughout this book, it's that we should be asking for and expecting more from the young people we are parenting.

But, first things first ...

In addition to navigating tough conversations, by the end of this book I will have shown you the factors that contribute to a teenager's ability to govern their *own* behaviour, so that you won't need to be as much of a director. In fact, that's *exactly* where we'll be focusing — on your teenagers' increasing ability to control their own behaviour and not just because you *said so*!

Below is a detailed outline of everything that I cover.

In **Part One** (Chapters 1 to 4) we'll look at the type of things you can assume is normal behaviour while living with a teenager, and what misbehaviour looks like. We will also look at how a teenager's challenging behaviour starts and develops. I'm not going to pull any punches here. I will outline some clear expectations you can have of your teenager that are entirely reasonable and shared by many other parents. And it won't matter which culture you're from; it will be commonsense for raising teenagers everywhere.

In **Part Two** (Chapters 5 to 7) we learn what professionals, such as pilots do in an emergency. Here's what they do: they learn *away* from the emergency to know what to do *in* an emergency. Knowing what other people do when things get hectic will help you learn by their example. Then we look at what you can do to 'hold your nerve' in a challenging or confronting situation, and how to keep things under control.

In **Part Three** (Chapters 8 to 11) we take a look at some case studies about how to successfully hold tough conversations with teenagers and come out the other side intact. We will also look at a previously road-tested mediation process for holding tough conversations. The good thing about using any kind of scripted process is that it can be adapted to suit a range of different environments and situations. You know, like when a violin player learns to play individual notes and then applies that learning to play a range of different music.

So, to get started, let's look at teenagers and the landscape through which they are journeying.

PART ONE

THE TEENAGE PARENTING LANDSCAPE

1

RAISING TEENAGERS THESE DAYS

Although most jobs come with some kind of job description, I haven't seen that many for raising teenagers. If I were to write down a job description for parents of teenagers, I'd say it's about three things:

» helping your teenager reach emotional maturity

» ensuring their wellbeing

» teaching them the difference between what's 'appropriate' and 'inappropriate' in behaviour.

So let's look at these one by one.

Helping your teenager reach emotional maturity

Scott Peck, a psychiatrist in the 1970s, put forward the idea that the degree to which individuals have reached maturity is reflected in the way they are able to balance their reactions to events. He reckoned a pretty good sign of adulthood is a person's ability to respond to frustrating events proportionally. Full maturity, he said, is tied up with how much we let our emotions unbalance us. And, if we can't work out how to balance our emotions and get things in proportion then maybe we have more maturing to do! For instance, we would fully expect that any of us might take exception to:

» someone sharply pulling out in front of us in their car

» someone pushing ahead of us in a queue

» someone acting dangerously around a person we love.

We might even get very upset about these things. However, what might at first glance look like someone setting out to deliberately annoy us, may not be the case at all once we get a chance to think about it. The person who pulls out in front of us in their car may be distracted by a baby in the back seat; the person who pushes ahead of us in a queue may have a sick mother at home, and the person who acts dangerously around someone we love may just not realize that what they are doing is dangerous. Many times it all depends on how we see it — and other factors we may not see at all. It's not useful to always jump to harsh conclusions. But that takes the ability to use perspective, and that in turn takes a level of maturity.

The ability to be able to weigh up events and put situations in perspective comes with maturity. And, here's the thing: when teenagers display behavioural problems, often what's happening is that they are just overreacting to a frustration. They have a disproportionate reaction to an event that might not warrant it.

Let's get back to Peck's theory for a minute. If someone pulls out in front of you in their car, in the scheme of frustrating or upsetting things, this might be classed as a 4/10 event. Depending on how you perceive it, it might actually evoke an 8/10 response. However, another event, such as a person in your family possibly being harmed, may be classed as a 9/10 event and require a

9/10 response. My interpretation of what Peck means is that not every event requires an 8/10 response, but often what we see in misbehaving teenagers is a 9/10 explosive reaction to 4/10 events if they let frustration take over.

Event   *Reaction*

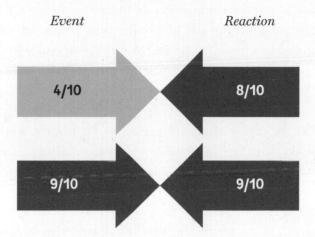

Peck would say that the balance between an event and a reaction to an event is a reflection of our level of maturity. It is about being able to adjust to situations that require us to react differently. Sure some situations require us to get cross — even really angry — while others require us to put a gentle handbrake on proceedings.

A big part of what we're trying to do as parents is to help teens get better at responding to things proportionally (i.e. when to get really cross or when to put the handbrake on gently so they can handle frustration more successfully). It's not the feeling that's the problem; it's how the feeling is being expressed.

Ensuring their wellbeing

When it comes to the ability to exert emotional control, you can lay money on you being able to manage yourself emotionally better than your teenager. Even more than this, if it comes to making a call about whether or not your teenager is crossing the line, you should trust your years of experience and your greater ability to coordinate all the necessary information to make the best decision.

If you see your teen developing a lifestyle that you can't stomach, you have the right to influence them. An adult's mature brain is better able to coordinate an array of information compared to a teenager's brain. (Not unlike when a new iPhone comes out as an improvement on the old one; as an adult, you're just better at weighing up elements of a situation like context and appropriateness than teenagers.)

I'm not saying adults are perfect — far from it, we will all make our fair share of mistakes — but as an adult you're going to size things up with more wisdom, experience and tolerance compared to your fifteen-year-old Joe or Joanne.

While we can assume that teenagers will develop better judgment the older they become, we should also assume that, just like children who don't know when it's time to go to bed (and need Mum or Dad to prompt them), teenagers need their mum and dad to make up for their *not-yet-complete* brain when making decisions. They need their parents to step in to look after their wellbeing. This means there are going to be times when you'll have to step in to ensure they are safe. This includes influencing teens in working out what are acceptable and unacceptable levels of risk in the things they want to do.

There are two types of influencers. The first type is those who 'project' their own view of the future onto their teenager, such as pressuring them to be a doctor, when all they really want to do is pursue music. The second type acts in what they feel is their teen's best interests. It's not always easy to distinguish between the two, but they are qualitatively different. The first tries to make a teenager in the image of something they want themselves, while the second supports and encourages their teens to be the best people they can be.

I want to offer three reasons why we should expect to *influence* our sons or daughters.

1. If you relinquish your role as an influencer *before* your teen is fully mature, you are ignoring the science of brain development. Numerous longitudinal studies, including those conducted by Dr Jay Giedd, the Chief of Brain Imaging at the US Institute of Mental Health, a man who has spent more than twenty years researching the adolescent brain, clearly show that teenagers are a *work-in-progress* and their brains are not fully mature until they are around age 24. This means that the part of their minds that can plan, prioritize and consider consequences is at best only three-quarters built from the ages of eleven to eighteen. Your brain, on the other hand, is complete and you generally can see things that they can't.

2. When we presume that teens can look after themselves without guidance from us or other adults, we succumb to a view that says that what we're offering is insignificant. When we do this, we are saying that all our years of experience, thought and adult maturity count for little. This is seldom the case.

3. If we give up our efforts to influence our teenager because it causes too much conflict and angst, we fool ourselves that it's more important to keep the peace than try to set reasonable expectations. We end up telling ourselves that it's all too hard to make a significant difference and they'll be leaving the family home soon enough. If there is a problem and we ignore it, but our son or daughter lives at home for longer than we anticipate, we relinquish an appropriate level of authority and integrity by living like this.

This last scenario is what I have seen the most — and it's probably the most debilitating position for parents. Relinquishing your *influencing* role is easy enough to do. Lots of parents want a hassle-free life. It's actually pretty common for parents to succumb. In such a situation they might say, 'I am aware that things with my daughter are not that great,' or 'I know I don't like what my son is doing, but I just hope *he'll grow out of it.*' But he seldom will — at least not on your watch — and not without some positive influencers in his life. I will be looking at what happens when teenagers are left to their own devices in regard to technology, sleep and alcohol in coming chapters but, suffice to say, these problems can be managed by having a good influencer in their lives.

Teaching them the difference between what's 'appropriate' and 'inappropriate' in behaviour

In his book *Essentialism*, author Greg McKeown says that in a digitally interconnected world people aren't learning how to discriminate between choices. In fact, I'd say that some teenagers haven't necessarily developed the antennae to figure out what is important from what isn't.

This spells trouble if we're talking about behaviour, because that can mean *anything* goes, while in even the most broad-minded of us, an anything-goes approach can be a recipe for disaster. Amy Alkon, the author of *Nice Manners for Good People Who Sometimes Say F*ck*, says that society today is moving faster and as such, we are losing a degree of common decency that goes with living closely with people we know. Historically, she says, our brains have become used to living with people. Somehow living less physically close with and to other people is reducing the level of respect we show them. In other words, we have lost a common decency and the good manners we used to show one another when we related more face to face.

One of the key roles of parents is to be guardians of good manners and acceptable behaviour in our teens, whether or not that is welcome. Instead of becoming a walking, talking guide to good manners, if you couch something in terms of whether it is socially appropriate — or not — you are likely to get your teen to listen to you. The word 'rule' is far more likely to get up any teenager's nose as opposed to evaluating something in terms of appropriateness. Appropriate implies that something is the same for the Smiths who live two doors down or for the cousins who live in the neighbouring suburb. It is something teens can relate to.

For instance, you might be telling your teenager it is *not* appropriate to:

>> bring their phone to the table when you are eating together

>> visit websites that you have deemed not okay — for example, suicide, radicalization, violent or abusive sites where people are not respected — especially when *you* are paying the internet bill!

>> distribute your family's private business to public scrutiny on Facebook, Twitter or other social media (no, this is not okay)

>> not let you know where they are or if they are going to be home late

>> just let you and your partner do all the work around the house while they do nothing to contribute.

You might also tell them it *is* appropriate to:

>> greet someone by shaking their hand firmly while looking them in the eye

- » spend ten minutes with adult visitors before they leave to then go and do their own thing
- » acknowledge somebody when they do something for you
- » pitch in by doing something such as bake a cake, tell a funny story at the dinner table or wash up occasionally
- » to act with kindness in their dealings with others. After all, most people are trying their best.

Establishing family guardrails

In the early 2000s, a US health company called KP HealthConnect began rolling out a record-keeping system, first in Hawaii, and then in other US states. It collected health information it envisaged would be used to improve patient outcomes for the entire United States. KP HealthConnect collected certain information from all the hospitals in a uniform way, so as to compare apples with apples (or *like* information with *like* information). However, the people collecting the information in all the different hospitals didn't collect the data in a uniform way. One hospital decided to collect information in one way and another hospital decided to collect information a different way. Before too long those apples became cumquats and rockmelons — and the information could not be compared. So, here's what they did.

KP HealthConnect decided to constrain the way information would be collected by putting 'guardrails' in place. This became known as its 'guardrail' strategy. It insisted that some 'non-negotiables' be put in place so that the majority of the information was collected in the same way — while some other additional information could be collected locally. The solution meant that some things were very important, while other things were less important and could be adjusted to local situations.

This analogy is just like you living with your teenager. You need to work out the few things that are 'non-negotiable' — the things that really matter — and let the rest go. While you might be able to accommodate differences in some of your teenager's behaviour, there are some values and behaviours you are not willing to accept. My advice to you is that you need to take the time to put these important *guardrails* in place — just enough so that your kids know what is 'non-negotiable' at your place — but not too many.

I realize that our teenagers will have different interests to us, but that doesn't mean that they can assume the behaviours and attitudes from some online world that do not fit with your family values. Sure, they might be entitled to have differing interests to us, but when the ugly side of those interests starts getting played out in your home and begin to affect how you live together, it's time to challenge that. It is not okay for your son, for instance, to be saying things like, 'Get your woman in order,' to their friends or even their elders, just because that is common parlance in the media they are hearing or watching. We do not live in this kind of society and nor is it appropriate, in a mature society, for young people to be subscribing to this type of talk, which only feeds misogyny.

And it's not okay, in my books, for young girls to be spending lots of their time on social media platforms like Instagram or Facebook trying to get as many 'likes' as they can so that they can then become mules for advertisers. Instagram, in particular, feeds this kind of obsessive use by teenagers, because young people can make money out of promoting goods and services if they have a threshold of followers. But we don't have to buy into this marketers' web and I don't think we should be letting our kids be seduced by it either.

The kind of non-negotiable value setting I'm talking about doesn't have to be a formal procedure, but it does have to be done. It's a bit like identifying the holding pattern you expect your teens to exist within while they live with you. Think of it as *making the invisible visible* — identifying family values that represent your lives together. You could, for example, say the following:

> » 'Guys, we love you, you know that don't you? But we live here as a family, not in some hotel come-and-go-as-you-like arrangement, so you'll need to talk to us about where you want to go, with whom, and when you plan to be home.'

> » 'We will provide for you as best we can. We expect that you will respect the people who live here. That means not whacking your sister and coming to us instead if something happens where you're tempted to hit her.'

> » 'Look guys, here's the deal. While you are living here, we expect you to live according to our family values — not like the ones on [the TV show] *Home and Away*. Our house is not the set of *Home and Away*. So, it's not okay for you to regularly make dramas out of little stuff.'

> » 'That may be the way that you see rappers speaking to other people, Joe, but they live a different life to us and I really don't want that kind of talk around here. Your sister is not 'a ho' and I don't want you to speak to her like that.'

I am not suggesting you should run your family like the von Trapps. Nor am I saying you should curtail your children's personal style. However, unless you have a good grasp of what's important versus what's not, you will find yourself relinquishing control when it's not necessary. You also run the risk of appearing wishy-washy about things you really need to be firm about. When you are wishy-washy with a temperamental teenager, not only will they not respect you, but you'll stand less chance of being able to influence them when you need to.

It's helpful to think about what the important baseline expectations are in your family. While such a list will differ from family to family, some common expectations might be:

- » We all have a right to live safely in our own home.
- » We are all entitled to be treated with respect.
- » We will all contribute to the general upkeep and day to day maintenance of the household.
- » We'll regularly spend *some* time together as a family.
- » You (adolescents) will work towards independence by attending school or training — and trying your best.

In essence

- » The job of raising teenagers is threefold: help them reach maturity by teaching them to balance their emotions, protect their wellbeing and prompt them about 'appropriate' and 'inappropriate' behaviour.
- » We know a teenager has crossed a line when it strains our family values or offends what we think is right.
- » Teenagers' obligations are to be respectful, to learn (either at school or at their job) and to make a contribution around the house.
- » Parents need to be clear about the tone of life they want to establish with their teenagers and to say, aloud, the family values and the behaviours they expect to be followed.

2.

WHAT TEENAGERS CAN AND CAN'T DO

A way of thinking about teenagers is to think of them as like boats. Yes, boats! Boats have *on-board* systems for navigation (a rudder, a motor, a compass) and *off-board* systems (weather reports, charts and satellites). A teenager's on-board system includes *some* ability to exert self-control and this should be steadily improving year on year. Therefore, we should rightly expect that a fifteen-year-old's ability to work out a proportional emotional response to a frustration will be better than a thirteen-year-old's, and a thirteen-year-old's ability will be better than a ten-year-old's and so on. That's the good news — and it's actually *really* good news — and it gives us something to rely on when we are trying to make improvements to a teenager's behaviour.

But teenagers are also like boats in that in order to function well they need *off-board* systems, such as Mum or Dad's provision of material goods or ongoing love and affection and, on occasion, their greater foresight to direct them. Not only is a parent's capacity to nurture a teenager important in helping them thrive, it can also play a role in stopping teenagers from crashing into the rocks!

Building a teenager's on-board capacity

It is possible to set up circumstances so that your teenager is more likely to control their *own* behaviour. In other words, they are getting to the stage where they should have to rely less on your explicit direction and more on their ability to control themselves. Let's face it — most self-respecting 15-year-olds give the *impression* that they can do it on their own anyway, notwithstanding relying on their parents for:

» their meals (breakfast, lunch, dinner)

» washing their clothes

» a roof over their heads

» putting their possessions away

» driving them to and from football/netball practice or piano/tennis lessons

» picking them up from parties

» giving them money for school excursions

» listening to how 'tough' their day was

» helping with homework

» mending their favourite jeans

» taking them to the doctor

» buying Christmas presents

» taking them on holidays

» paying for social outings

» buying takeaway food

» cleaning their shoes.

(When I read over this list I am reminded of the line in the Monty Python movie *The Life of Brian* that asked, 'What did the Romans ever do for us?' In the same manner we could ask, 'What did *parents* ever do for their kids?')

While some teens vary in their ability to show emotional control, and this can be dependent on a whole range of things such as hormones, lack of sleep and levels of stress they are under, there are some things you can do to help them help themselves when it comes to increasing their on-board ability to be more flexible.

Psychologist and author of the bestselling book *Emotional Intelligence,* Daniel Goleman refers to three elements of emotional flexibility (the capacity to harness our emotional selves):

» *paying attention* to emotions within oneself

» *tracking feelings* (sensations, feelings and fleeting thoughts) within oneself

» *managing emotions* by amplifying some emotions and lessening others or choosing not to let an emotion drive a behaviour.

It's a hierarchy. None of us can do the third thing — manage our emotions — unless we're able to pay *inward attention* and *notice* these emotions. Of course, there is a subtle difference between these abilities, but Goleman, says that unless we can do the first two actions, it's very difficult to do the third and manage our emotions. Developing emotional intelligence, Goleman says, is about navigating your way through emotional difficulties.

Self-control begins at age four

There are lots of times when we become frustrated by what happens to us, but that doesn't mean we will lose control. Teenagers are no different — albeit just a bit less sophisticated in handling frustration. But, if you're a teenager you don't get a 'get-out-of-jail-free card' by virtue of age. Being a teenager does not mean you can misbehave every other day, whenever you feel like it. More than that, we don't want our son or daughter to fall prey to dark moods, when circumstances don't warrant it.

Managing behaviour in teenagers has a lot to do with helping them get better at using the skills Goleman is referring to. It is entirely reasonable for you to believe that they can *constrain, restrain, pull back, hold-up-there, listen* or *wait* until you have finished talking.

Teenagers, in fact, have had signs of an ability to 'hold fire' with their emotions since they were four. In the 1960s psychologist Walter Mischel devised an experiment where he asked very young children, (some were as young as four) to wait alone in a room with a marshmallow on a table in front of them. If they could wait until a researcher returned they could have two marshmallows. The now-famous 'marshmallow' experiments showed one-third of the children were able to wait the required fifteen minutes to get their second marshmallow. This experiment showed that even at the age of four, some children could *restrain* themselves.

In the video footage of the experiment, the children showing restraint did not look that comfortable. They can be seen grimacing, struggling or squirming to maintain control. But what the experiment discovered was that some children were able to resist the temptation by *shifting their attention* or by *distracting* themselves away from the marshmallow. They demonstrated enough mental flexibility to shift their thoughts even when they felt a certain level of frustration.

When we see our teenagers struggling to restrain their emotions in a similar manner, we needn't jump in to protect them. They might look uncomfortable, scrunch up their face and look as if they are wrestling internally. In fact, it's *in* these struggling moments that much learning is going on. It's important to let them have these developmental experiences, otherwise they won't practise using their mind in this way. That is, they won't learn how to harness their own initial reactions. It's only with practice that the part of the mind that does the restraining will be able to function.

I know it may sound odd that a psychologist would suggest

that you should purposefully let your children experience discomfort, but I am not alone. Here's what Dr Dan Siegel, author of the book *Parenting From the Inside Out,* says parents should be doing:

> In order to do this [let your child mentally weigh things up] a parent needs to be able to tolerate the tension and discomfort that a child may experience when a parent sets a limit. If a parent cannot tolerate a child's being upset it is very difficult for the child to regulate her emotions.

The same thing applies with teenagers. If you don't let them struggle with frustration when they're not getting their way, they won't as readily develop the ability to tolerate distress. What can happen to some young people who don't learn to tolerate *some* distress is that they end up resorting to mind-altering substances to help them cope. Some may end up doing that anyway, but unless young people are helped to tolerate a bit of having to wrestle with competing urges, they won't get the practice. If they don't practise, the part of their mind that *restrains* won't develop as well.

In fact, when young people are sent to drug rehabilitation centres, one of the key aims of therapy is to help them manage distress. It's often when teenagers haven't learnt to tolerate distress that they resort to drugs in the first place. So, the treatment is aimed at resolving the problem at its core. If they can learn to tolerate a certain amount of frustration or manage it, then they're on the road to recovery.

Distress tolerance practice is an important part of growing up and learning how to respond to a frustrating event. But, if there is no practice, our mind's ability to wrestle with frustration does not improve. The four-year-olds in the marshmallow experiment displayed an ability to wrestle with their first impulse (or hold back from eating the marshmallow). According to Siegel, this is known as a healthy type of inhibition and it's a necessary part of developing the ability to show restraint. It's also a sign, as Peck would say, of improving maturity, and a reminder to us that our job is to help our teens to respond to frustrating events proportionally. Holding back is just a part of life and happens everywhere from waiting in line, taking turns to speak and putting a hand up in school.

Helping teens think flexibly

We know that from a developmental perspective, the ability to wrestle with initial impulses gets better with age — that much is clear. What corresponds with this increased ability is the capacity to think *flexibly* — to either magnify or lessen feelings of distress or frustration. You can help teenagers develop this flexibility.

When I was learning to be a psychologist one of my psychiatrist supervisors pointed out that what *defines* misbehaviour in teenagers is nearly always to do with a lack of self-regulation. In other words, a teenager's difficult behaviour is usually related to his or her ability to exert *self-control*, independent of any diagnosis they might have.

I have seen many young people with behavioural problems who were somewhat rigid. They suffered what I call 'brain lock': they locked onto certain ways of behaving and they failed to take into account the *context* they were in or perceive any lasting consequences. What happened was that they ratcheted up their misbehaviour. They could have scaled their behaviour *down*, but they didn't. More often than not, they didn't keep control.

Looking at misbehaviour in this way, rather than looking through a prism of diagnosis, made me focus on the *behaviour* itself and how to change it. The famous DSM-5, a manual of mental health disorders which professionals use to identify and diagnose conditions like attention problems or oppositional disorders, does not suggest how to *manage* behaviour. All it does is offer a framework for considering a problem.

The majority of teenagers' behaviour correlates to the extent to which they have or haven't figured out how to harness their emotions. Remember what Goleman said? It's about identifying, tracking and then managing emotions. As we have seen, helping teenagers get better at managing their feelings in proportion to a frustrating event is a sign of maturity. It's just as much about encouraging them to realize when to speak up or shout out as it is in encouraging them to realize when it's best to retreat or yield to another. I will cover how you can help teenagers develop this flexibility in more detail in Chapter 3.

Why parents don't take action

In my career, I have seen parents who've pretty much lost control at home even though their children are only twelve or thirteen years old. They don't want to drive their child away by broaching a tough subject, and they are willing to compromise their values in order to avoid an uncomfortable conversation. Often this is because they are afraid their child will rebuke them. This is a big issue that parents struggle with. It appears that many more parents want to be 'liked' by their teenagers than a generation ago. I certainly know that my parents did not worry about whether or not I *liked* them as much as many parents do these days. Truly, whether or not my parents thought I liked them was secondary in their minds to whether or not *I* was behaving myself. And let me tell you, their attitude did not lessen my love for them.

We shouldn't just ignore poor behaviour by excusing it as a stage or because we don't want to intervene. Some behaviour is beyond the pale — and needs to be dealt with. We've become squeamish about saying no, somehow believing that our family's stability will be threatened if we take a stance on a particular matter. It takes courage to say no and it's not surprising that we give in to a teenager's way of doing things because we don't want them to get angry or push back.

In the next chapter we'll look at some external factors which not only affect your teenagers' ability to manage their emotions but over which you *have* control. If you hold the reins in these matters, you can make a difference to your teenager's behaviour. The link between a happier life with your teenager, and your capacity to influence them, is worth unpacking and we will look at when and where *your influence* can make a big difference.

In essence

» A good way of thinking about teenagers, and your relationship with them, is to think of them as being like boats. Boats have on-board systems and off-board systems that help them operate well.

» Often teenagers have trouble getting a hold of their emotional selves, but parents can help them to recognize the feelings they have, and help them not be driven by them.

» Teenagers need our help to keep perspective and to guide them towards emotional maturity.

» Teenagers will get progressively better at controlling their feelings as a function of their age. Even so, there are some things parents can do to accelerate their ability to exert self-control.

» Learning to *restrain, constrain* and *wait there* is a habit of self-control that needs to be practised.

» Unless you can tolerate some distress at seeing your teens struggle during these times (when you are correcting them), they won't get the practice they need to develop distress tolerance. A common issue for parents is to not take action due to fear of creating anger and resentment in their child.

3

MIND MAINTENANCE FOR TEENAGERS

In the previous chapter we talked about the ability that teens have to harness and manage their emotions. A major task of being able to manage distressing emotions is figuring out how to tolerate them for a *long enough time* to make a good choice. This capacity to tolerate distressing feelings without succumbing to them is being developed during the teenage years. The place where this happens is in the prefrontal area of our brain called the prefrontal middle cortex. Psychologists call this capacity *premeditation*. It's having a feeling like anger and — even while having it — knowing you have a choice about how you will respond. You can amplify it or lessen it, you can act on it or you can just tolerate it. Any or all of these things are possible, but the bottom line is you can *choose* to do this by using your ability to premeditate. By understanding premeditation — and a teenager's ability to use it — we can understand a lot about so-called *difficult* behaviour.

In order for the prefrontal cortex to operate well, the right conditions have to be met. As a parent, you can do a lot to provide the *right* conditions.

Before we go on, let's summarize for a moment. You'll recall:

» Most *difficult* behaviour in teenagers is to do with the lack of ability to self-regulate emotions.

» This self-regulatory ability improves year-on-year as a teenager's brain develops.

» The part of the brain that does the coordinating and harnessing of emotions (i.e. premeditation) is the prefrontal cortex.

I have talked about how improvements in a teenager's ability to exert self-control is related to his or her stage of development. That is clearly something *you can't* control. You also can't control your child's temperament and genes. I'm sure we have all seen children from the same family, raised in the same circumstances, who are very different from one another. What I want to talk about now though are those things you *can* control.

The use of constraints to enable flexibility

We care for our teenage children on a whole lot of levels: by providing good food and clothing and providing 'a home'. But it's also important to look after and encourage their mental flexibility by having constraints in place. In other words, you can organize things at home to affect your teen's ability to use their mind to work optimally.

Constraints are not necessarily a bad thing. We regulate employers to care for their staff through health and safety regulations, by getting them to contribute to superannuation and by requiring them to organize reasonable work hours — all good things. Constraints in the form of laws also help us. For example, on the roads, speed limits, traffic lights and police help us constrain what we do in order to keep traffic flowing and accidents to a minimum. And racial vilification laws stop us attacking someone on the basis of their race, thereby promoting tolerance and social harmony.

If you want your teenager to react less and use his or her emotional intelligence more, you'll need to organize some things you *can* control. It's to these factors that we now turn. An incredibly important mind-maintenance issue is to influence things in your home to maximize their ability to self-regulate emotions. Factors that you, as parents, can influence include:

» ensuring they get proper sleep
» balancing the use of technology in their lives with other activities
» holding off giving them alcohol (and drugs).

If you get *these* things right, you can make an enormous difference to your teenager's ability to premediate and to their ability to think flexibly. This will translate into them being able to self-regulate their emotions.

Ensuring they get proper sleep

Professor Dorothy Bruck from Australia's Sleep Health Foundation says the US guidelines, based on a review of 312 studies, complements recent Australian research. Berkeley University academic Matthew Walker found that, 'without [proper] sleep, the brain reverted back to more primitive patterns of activity... in that it was unable to put emotional experiences into context and produce controlled, appropriate responses'. Mmm ... I think I've seen some teenagers behaving in this space.

When some young people are feeling anxious, it's often related to a lack of sleep. The symptoms of anxiety — the worry, the fretting and the uncontrolled negative thinking — are not being kept in check by a rested mind. Anxiety can 'cycle'. This is where a young person can't get off the treadmill of worry. If you've ever come across an anxious teenager my first suggestion is have a look at how much sleep they are getting. You might be surprised to know that a lot of what we *see* as anxiety has to do with a lack of timely, uninterrupted sleep.

When we are asleep, more blood is supplied to the areas of our brain other than the premeditating and coordinating prefrontal cortex. Author and psychologist Norman Doidge says that during sleep we experience increased activity in the hind part of our brains, producing vivid sexual, survival and aggressive dreams. In this state, our impulses are amplified and not held in check by our prefrontal cortex, which shows less activity (less blood supply goes there) because *it's asleep*. That's why we have those fantastic dreams. Our dreams are *not* controlled by the *civilizing* influence of the prefrontal cortex. When we wake up we may not be too forthcoming about the content of these dreams!

Sleep is important

» Teenagers need more sleep than adults.

» They need at least 8.5 to 10 hours sleep.

» Proper sleep helps the mind to recuperate and recuperation helps stem anxiety.

What happens for any of us who are sleep-deprived is that the ability to apply mental 'brakes' is affected. We can find ourselves irritable and short-tempered. The part of our mind that coordinates and weighs up options does not function as well. This part of the mind needs regular *recuperative rest* in order to work properly. If the recuperation doesn't occur, its ability to be the coordinator and exercise restraint can be affected. It's that simple. This lack of rest can result in a cranky-pants teenager that you have to deal with. For many parents who are living with tired, irritable teenagers — and that's a lot of parents — it can be an exhausting state of affairs. Any attempt to reason or set limits won't be very successful because the pre-requisites for teenage self-control (adequate rest, the ability to pay attention and think flexibly) are compromised by poor sleep habits. More often than not, irritable teenagers will also tend to give a disproportionate reaction to a minor imposition. This is because their prefrontal cortex, already taxed by a lack of regenerative rest, *can't* exert enough control to coordinate a mature response.

By the way, with regard to sleep, computers, tablets and smart phones emit a light that stops melatonin — a hormone that helps us fall asleep — from working. The artificial light produced by digital screens, which is often called blue light, has a disruptive effect on sleep. It interferes with the body's circadian rhythm, the 24-hour biological clock that controls our sleep–wake cycle. Fortunately, there are free apps to reduce blue light. The circadian screen adjustment app f.lux is available for use on iPhone, iPad and Apple computers. The app will adjust the blue light for you at sunset every day. For Android devices try a similar app called Twilight. Setting devices on flight mode will also lessen the strength of blue light from electronic devices.

Teenagers who are tired are more likely to misbehave because the part of their mind is not getting the regular maintenance it needs. New planes need to go in for a service to be airworthy. My view is that teenagers need good rest to behave like human beings!

When we're talking about parenting and helping teenagers gain control over their behaviour, we ignore teenagers' sleep needs at our peril.

What you can do

» Teens need between 8.5 and 10 hours sleep at night. Prompt them to get ready for bed early enough to ensure they get the right amount of sleep.

» An obvious no-no is coffee and exercise close to bedtime; they will stimulate anyone.

» Insist on no technology in bedrooms (including phones) after a certain time, usually an hour before sleep time. Set up a charging basket in the kitchen or another room where everyone's digital devices go overnight.

» Block social networking and email at the router level and set teens' handheld devices to switch off at a set time. (For directions on how to locate these apps, see the Resources on page 198)

Balancing the use of technology with other activities

Closely associated with a teenager's ability — or lack of ability — to make their mind work is their use of technology. When I talk to parents about technology and its place in the home, I refer to the internet as an invited guest, not an assumed resident. This ultimately means that although you may not be able to control what happens 'out there' on the net, you *can* control what happens in your home — and you should, because it has BIG implications for protecting your teenager's wellbeing. There is also growing evidence that aspects of technology, such as playing video games or interacting on social networks such as Facebook for extended periods of time, affects teenagers' mental health. Craig Anderson, the Director of the Center for the Study of Violence at Iowa State University, states that there are new studies which 'link violent video games — and to a certain extent, total screen time — to attention-related problems and, ultimately, to aggression'. Anderson and colleagues found that while playing action video games is associated with better visuo-spatial attention skills, it is also linked to a reduction in proactive cognitive control. 'These studies are the first to link violent video game play with both beneficial and harmful effects within the same study,' Anderson says.

The digital games of today are more graphic and, in some cases, more realistic than games of yesteryear. These games frequently put the player in the active role of a character who makes decisions to commit acts of violence. The player of the game is involved at a psychological level in killings, rapes, assaults and other criminal activity. We don't actually know the full impact of this exposure, especially on developing brains, but it is likely to be desensitizing players to violence and, to some extent, normalizing violent behaviour.

And, before you think I am overstating the effects of violent gaming, consider this. For the past 30 years we have trained commercial pilots in simulators so that they know how to behave in different real-life situations. In other words, pilots use virtual situations *away* from an event to learn how to behave *in* the event. What we are seeing in some children and teenagers who play games like *Call of Duty* and *Grand Theft Auto* is an increase in visual skills and hand–eye coordination, but a decrease in an ability to hold back or appropriately inhibit some behaviour, especially aggressive impulses. That's indeed a worry when it comes to teenage misbehaviour.

While some parents and professionals might wish to see violent video games banned, just as our society prohibits other dangerous drugs and firearms, realistically, this is unlikely to happen any time soon.

What you can do

» Take an active interest in your children's digital world and pay close attention to the activities they engage in. Set limits and provide a positive example of responsible digital use. If we want our kids to limit their time on their phones, then we have to limit our time on our phones as well.

» Set limits on the amount of time spent using technology. Any more than three hours a day online is probably too much, but this is an individual preference. Any usage should not come at the expense of teens sleeping properly, learning at school, engaging in face-to-face time with their friends and family, and enjoying other social or sporting activities.

» Teens need to be taught that real-world interactions come before virtual ones. Online connections are no substitute for real friends and real social activities.

» Establish a set of guidelines for the use of technology at home and outside the home. These guidelines need to include limiting the use of technology, protecting personal privacy, dealing with cyber bullying and online etiquette. Children also need to know what to do if they encounter inappropriate content.

» Talk to your teen about their online research for school, their social connections or the games they are playing. Discuss situations that you have concerns about.

» While you should initially trust that your teen is using web resources appropriately, if you find out they're logging on to any internet-nasties (suicide sites, porn or eating disorder sites) you can always set up a filter like K9. It's free and, I am told, virtually un-hackable.

Holding off from giving them alcohol (and drugs)

I'm going to make this section short and sweet. I don't claim to be an expert in this area, but Paul Dillon, who is the Director of Drug and Alcohol Research Training Australia (DARTA), says that when he first began working in the field twenty years ago, the advice given to parents was to teach their teenagers to learn to *drink responsibly* by modelling responsible drinking behaviour at home. He told me the newest research is *now* saying that we should *stop* teenagers drinking for as long as possible.

It's always tricky for parents to know how to manage this issue. In the current social context how to contain our teenagers' drinking or drug use can become quite fraught. On the one hand, teenagers will always want to push the boundaries and seek new experiences. And, I suppose we have to be realistic. You can't just assume that your teenager will not succumb to peer pressure to experiment with alcohol and drugs. In the end the pressure might be too strong and the pleasure too much to resist! The question then is what consideration should we give to this issue, and what should we do to protect our teens' wellbeing?

I have met a variety of parents who have become confused as to what is best to do in this area. From what I have seen, there are three main types of parents:

1. The 'It didn't hurt me' types.
2. The 'European thinkers' who say that giving teenagers some alcohol under guidance at home is better than letting them sneak it outside of home.
3. The 'boundary setters' who won't let it happen.

Paul Dillon suggests that the thinking of the first two types of parents is not the best way to tackle teen drinking. It appears that young people who drink early in life are far more likely to develop poor drinking habits in their adult life. There is no evidence that giving them alcohol under supervision teaches them to drink responsibly. The main message from the research is that the parents who set clear boundaries for their children in relation to alcohol and drugs are usually more successful in influencing their children's behaviour in the long term.

Drinkswise Australia have put together an excellent strategy for helping parents to cope with teens and alcohol, and I have included it below.

Delaying the introduction of alcohol for as long as possible starts at home — it's one of the most important things you can do as a parent.

Is it okay to let your kids drink at home?

While parents have differing views on this subject, there is no strong evidence to suggest that providing alcohol to your child at home teaches them to drink responsibly. Instead, behaviours are often learnt by teens watching parents and other role models with alcohol.

Research also shows that teens are less likely to drink if parents communicate they don't want them drinking, don't provide alcohol, and set rules and boundaries, as well as consequences if the rules are broken.

Dealing with a drunken teen

While social trends have seen a spike in teen binge drinking, the more informed you are, the better positioned you are to guide them through this challenging journey.

If your teen comes home intoxicated, you have a problem that needs to be dealt with quickly. It's normal to feel disappointed, but it's also not the time to overreact. As a parent, it's up to you to take control and manage the situation appropriately. You have to be firm and decisive in what to do next.

What to do if your teen comes home drunk

Look out for the signs. You'll likely be able to smell it on their breath or clothing.

Explain your concerns about drinking and the range of risks involved. They may not agree but they need to understand where you're coming from.

Set clear boundaries.

Try to find out what's led to this incident — it may not be 'just a stage'.

Make sure your teen knows you will always be there for them, whatever happens.

Wait until morning to discuss the situation. Put them to bed only once they've sobered up and let them know you'll talk to them later. Hopefully you'll be much calmer and they'll be feeling slightly hungover and more likely to accept your opinion and guidance.

Seek help from your GP or health professional if you're worried it's becoming regular behaviour.

Taken from *https://www.drinkwise.org.au/parents/how-to-deal-with-teen-drinking/#*

By taking steps to manage your teenager's sleep, to limit technology or your teen's use of alcohol, it is possible for you to improve their mind's ability to think flexibly and to have them accommodate some boundaries as they live with you. These three issues are three lifestyle issues that you can control — and doing so will make a big difference to a teenager's ability to manage their emotions.

In the next chapter, I'll describe the importance of not hassling your teenager when you don't need to so that you can protect your relationship. By sorting behaviour into types, you can tailor your responses to them to work out when you should intervene and to decide what you probably should take action about. Not all behaviour is created equal and there is some behaviour that crosses the line in anyone's language that you will need to actively manage.

In essence

>> We need to help our teenagers develop their *on-board* systems to better enable their ability to self-regulate emotions and control impulsive behaviour.

>> Teenagers will get progressively better — not worse — at controlling their feelings as they mature. Even so, there are some things we can do to optimize this ability.

>> There are three aspects of your home life you can control: the amount of sleep your teenagers get, their use of technology and their use of alcohol.

4

THE NATURE OF DIFFICULT BEHAVIOUR IN TEENAGERS

It can be tricky to maintain an ongoing positive relationship with some teenagers, who are pushing the boundaries and seeking out ever new experiences. Teens themselves are getting used to the changes happening in their body. Getting used to the new skin in which they find themselves can be a tough ask, what with hormones, increasing demands at school and the exacting expectations of social life all playing a part in making the adjustments even trickier. All the more important, then, to be somewhat forgiving and accommodating of your teen's moodiness and occasionally painful-to-watch behaviour. It's crucial then to only have haggles with them about the serious behaviour that really matters so as not to get into unnecessary power struggles.

I have seen a lot of families over my career and I would have to say that the most important part of being able to positively influence a teenager's life has to do with having more *good* experiences with them than bad ones. The marriage counsellors of the world have long known that relationships generally don't falter because couples fight; they tend to fail because couples don't build ongoing positive interactions into the fabric of their lives together — quite separate to the fact that they might fight occasionally. Having arguments over issues, therefore, is not as important as having shared, meaningful experiences.

As far as your teenager is concerned, that involves finding ways to connect with them through shared experiences. Joanne Fedler in her book on raising teenagers, *Love in the Time of Contempt*, says that we should always be connecting (her ABC) with our teenagers to insure against the times when we may need to be tough with them.

Clearly there are many ways to be involved. Playing sports together, going to the gym, cooking meals or building something together are just some of the activities that can be used as opportunities to 'turn towards' your teen. You can also use these times to encourage your teen to feel good about their developing skills and abilities. Teenagers will often be more positive towards their parents if they feel good about themselves. You can help build their self-confidence and resilience by helping them feel competent in the world. Below is a list of the types of things you can do to encourage a positive relationship. Some of them might seem like 'no brainers' but I think they are still worth mentioning:

» Set up regular times for doing routine activities or joining in on more spontaneous occasions to talk with your kids about what's going on in their lives. Some examples include kicking a football, walking the family dog, watching a funny movie or going to the beach. Many parents whose children are now grown up say that some of the most intimate times they have had with their children have been in the car while they were driving somewhere together.

» Look for the *good* they do — and tell them.

» Acknowledge when they have put effort into something worthwhile.

» Encourage them to help around the house and thank them when they do.

» Encourage them to join in family activities occasionally, and tell them how important it is to you that everyone makes an effort.

» Teach them living skills, such as how to cook, how to use household appliances like the washing machine and vacuum cleaner. (Good luck with that one!)

» Take an interest in their hobbies and friends ... and join in when you are allowed!

» Help them put together a résumé and make a plan for finding a part-time job. Support them in learning new skills and encourage them to 'have a go'.

If you notice your adolescent is down or upset, find a quiet time to ask them if there is anything you can help with. If they feel there is a problem they *can't* discuss with you, remind them that there are other people who can help — friends of the family, teachers, school counsellors, doctors or even telephone help lines.

While teenagers can bring verve to our lives, they can also bring sadness and worry. They are struggling to make sense of the world. While this may not translate into them being the nicest people to live with at times, it needn't mean you can't remember their good points — even if these are a while back. Sometimes teenagers aren't always the best reporters of 'who' they are. You may know them perhaps better than they know themselves, which means you can observe their good points.

Apart from wanting to suggest to you some ways that you can invest in your relationship with your teenager (already covered in many other good books in this area), I want to suggest to you a way to sort behaviour so that you won't unnecessarily hassle them about the small stuff.

Sort out behaviour so that you won't hassle them

When I meet parents facing a problem with their teenager's behaviour, I'd have to say they are mainly facing problems *containing* their teenager's behaviour. I have seen parents who are completely confused about *what* their son or daughter is doing. The best thing they feel they can do is hold on for the ride, and try to ensure that their child's wellbeing is not too affected while they figure out what to do next. It can be a scary time for many parents while they're watching this go on.

Unfortunately, many 'misbehaving' teenagers behave as if nobody is watching — which is kind of lovely if you're dancing, but not quite as great if your teenager is beginning to routinely reject your authority. Sometimes it feels terribly difficult to intervene, as we love our children and don't want to upset them or the harmony at home. Sometimes we also don't know when to intervene, or if a problem is worth getting upset over.

Most misbehaviour in young people usually starts at one point in time, and develops from there, either out of habit or because the circumstances reinforced it, or both. It is often the case that difficult behaviour in teenagers gets *more* difficult as they grow older, partly because they are becoming physically bigger and also because they have a greater intellectual capacity to challenge our values, logic and authority.

When young people are diagnosed with oppositional problems, usually their behaviour has been years in the making. Sorry, that's the bad news. And, any attempt to re-shape behaviour is going to take time and effort. While I will show you several ways in which you can modify a teenager's behaviour, the issue is that these patterns can be hard to shift. This is not to say that your efforts won't be rewarded — but you have to be realistic.

Set yourself small, manageable goals at first.

If things *aren't* going so well at home, you are probably facing two types of behaviour problems. The first sort is where you feel compelled to act immediately when something *startling* happens — like when your teenager stays out way too late or they've raided your drinks cabinet.

The second type of problem, and probably the more common, is where you're seeing your teen do something for the umpteenth dozen time that annoys the hell out of you and you've realized that this time you're *not* willing to let it go. This type of problem tends to aggregate. Like the proverbial snowball, it grows until you reach a point where it's all too much, and you have to do something. You may not be too clear about what to do, but you're pretty clear *something* has to be done.

In this section I will show you how to sort out what is annoying but minor behaviour (behaviour that you could ignore), wanted behaviour (behaviour that you want to instill in them, teach or prompt them to do) and more serious, unacceptable behaviour (behaviour you can't let go). Sorting behaviour into one of these three categories will help you know what to do when you next encounter this behaviour.

The main benefit of doing this sorting task is that it will cut your parenting job in half. I mean it. If you do this job well, you'll feel less hassled and so will your son or daughter. I have done this sorting exercise with over 7500 people directly and close to 25,000 people indirectly via the professionals I have trained. By all accounts it has made one of the biggest differences to problematic teenage behaviour at home. Just by sorting behaviour, parents are able to get a better perspective on what is happening with their kids. They are able to see what they can ignore and what they need to do something about.

There are four other benefits to sorting out our teenagers' behaviour:

» **So we can focus on a few key behaviours.** I've seen *a lot* of parents who do this. They 'fan the flames' by constantly pulling teenagers up on all sorts of things. This means their teenagers get lots of attention and respond, be it in a positive or negative way. But if we treat every behaviour with the same level of intensity, we can unintentionally reward children for misbehaviour. Then we're snookered. We can't *not* do something, but we set up a pattern of giving attention to all annoying behaviour.

» **So we don't ignore behaviour that we *should* respond to and end up exploding.** This is called *volcano parenting*, and it happens when parents put off ... and put off ... and put off doing anything about their children's misbehaviour until they are so irritated they snap. Paying this kind of attention to children sends them a mixed message. It's like saying that sometimes their behaviour matters and other times it doesn't.

» **So we can respond consistently.** When we sort our children's behaviour we can be more consistent in our reactions. We end up with a series of responses to behaviours that we have created at a calm time, rather than in the heat of an argument. Then we can respond according to what our children *are actually doing*.

» **So we can be more flexible, less stressed parents.** By sorting behaviours, we can choose to either ignore or manage them. Not every behaviour requires us to do something about it — so we can relax a little more. Not every behaviour requires us to use the same parenting tools to manage it, either. After a while, realizing that we have this kind of flexibility will result in less stress and make our parenting role more enjoyable.

Sorting behaviour is well worth the effort so you can reduce future dramas. But before we sort, let's get some *reminders* in place first.

First, we know that the vast majority of teenagers will get through to adulthood without major injury or landing in prison. This contradicts the important role of parents. Despite what we do, they will probably be okay. In fact, I love the title of Celia Lashlie's book *He'll Be Okay* for that reason. Celia says is if you have done a lot of hard yards early on, you can mostly hold on to the realistic belief that, even if things get pretty ugly during teenage years, most problems will iron themselves out over the medium term. If you provide your son or daughter with a nurturing framework, love them, look after them and influence them at appropriate times, they'll most likely do okay, even if they are currently a bit on the wild side.

Second, if we accept that teenagers have reached a point in their development where they *should* be better able to look after themselves, compared to when they were younger, we can also be comforted in the knowledge that they should be *better* at looking after themselves as they get older. That doesn't mean we should 'let go' in the sense of giving up. But it does mean that you will need to intervene less frequently as they reach maturity.

Third, there are some things that they will do that we don't need to get too het up about, because in the bigger scheme of things these issues might just come down to preferences.

Sorting behaviour is easy

One of the main tasks involved in sorting behaviour is to work out the difference between normal teenage behaviour and other behaviour that you need to deal with.

Your teenagers probably know precisely what buttons to push to get a reaction from you and you'd have to be super human to resist the barrage that they might hurl at you. Sometimes teenagers can be relentlessness in their pursuit of an advantage and frequently quite rude. This doesn't mean they are out of control or that they're bad kids. It just means that they are looking for a way to get you off their back — entirely normal and, as it turns out, entirely manageable.

For example, ever heard these words coming out of your teenager's mouth?

» 'If you got a life, you wouldn't be so concerned about mine.'

» 'You make a drama out of everything.'

» 'That's so old school; you're so out of touch!'

» 'You make my life a misery.'

» 'No one else's parents think like you do.'

» 'Sean's parents let him do anything he wants.'

If you're a step-parent you might have heard (or fear that one day you will hear) these kinds of comments:

» 'You're not my real father/mother.'

» 'I hate you; you've got no right to tell me what to do.'

» 'You're just a *visitor* here.'

» 'You just want to spoil my fun; I never liked you anyhow.'

Sorting behaviour can really help clarify where a problem lies in relation to other problems and therefore give you a guide on how to respond to it.

Observe, identify, write down and sort behaviours

Sorting involves four steps:

1. *Observe* your teenagers' different behaviours.

2. *Identify* what they are doing, without trying to explain it.

3. *Write down* what they are doing.

4. *Sort* what they are doing into categories.

Steps 1–3:

Observing something then identifying it means taking note of just what we see or hear, such as, 'He's yelling' or 'She rolls her eyes'. We don't need to add our own interpretations, like, 'He's a brat' or 'She's being hard to get along with'. Interpretations tell us how we feel about what our children are doing, but do not actually say what they are doing. So the first steps involve observing your children's behaviour and writing it down, while being careful not to interpret it.

Step 4:

The next step is to sort the behaviour into different categories. I use three categories, which are:

» ABNS (annoying but not serious): this is behaviour that you will ignore.

» Wanted behaviour that you want to instil, teach or prompt

» Can't-let-that-one-go: behaviour that needs active management.

ABNS — annoying but not serious behaviour that you will ignore

One person wisely put it that a big part of parenting teenagers is learning what to overlook. To lessen your teenage parenting dramas it's important to pay the 'right' level of attention to the right behaviour. Behaviour you can ignore can also be described as 'small fish' — things you can explain to yourself as part of your son's or daughter's *preferences*. These might include: their choice of clothes, music and their way of talking with their friends.

As I have already said, not all of teenagers' behaviour requires intervention by us. While we may not *like* some of their choices, we can live with them. Knowing the difference between the things an adolescent does that are a normal and quirky part of being a teenager and other big ticket issues is critical in order to avoid unnecessary scuffles. By not paying attention to small fish, we can keep our relationship intact so if a bigger fish comes along, we won't be seen by our teens as just 'hassling' them.

Suffice to say that different types of behaviour require different parent responses. In this case, when you see small fish, your action is non-action, meaning no sarcasm, no head flicks, no grimacing and no shaking your head — nothing.

Examples of behaviour we ignore:

> » Untidy room
> » Low-grade rudeness
> » Being grumpy
> » Choice of clothes
> » Pouting
> » Response of 'Whatever'

Wanted behaviour that you want to instil, teach or prompt

This is any kind of behaviour you'd like to see more of. It might be starting homework without being reminded, cleaning up the kitchen after snacking or doing their jobs around the house without being asked. Wanted behaviour involves having the reasonable belief that your teenager will do 'something' to contribute at home. You may have to prompt them (a more benign form of nagging) to get them to be consistent, but I think it's a fair enough call, especially if they're getting pocket money.

You can help generate this kind of behaviour by breaking down tasks into bite-sized bits, to prompt them when it's inappropriate to behave in a certain way and by encouraging them to put effort into things that you believe will help improve their sense of competency.

As we talked about in Chapter 1 it is possible and, I think, necessary for you to influence your teen in positive ways: to teach them about what is important in social situations; to require that they tell you where they are going; to follow through on what you say you are going to do, and generally influence them from time to time about what is appropriate behaviour in a given circumstance.

Examples of wanted behaviour:

> A regular contributor to household chores
> Eating with the family regularly
> Putting dirty clothes in the washing basket
> Communicating their whereabouts
> Being a 'willing' helper

Can't-let-that-one-go behaviour

These kinds of behaviours are ones that cross the line, interfere with your family life or are unsafe or reckless. These are the more serious kinds of behaviour that undermine relationships or expose teenagers to unacceptable risks. If these behaviours are not stopped, they are likely to have a negative impact on relationships with others or their health, or that of others. They are not acceptable and they need you (the parent) to intervene. Strategic intervening involves you sitting down with them and having a tough conversation — something we'll be looking at more closely in coming chapters.

Examples of can't-let-that-one-go behaviours

>> Swearing at others

>> High-grade rudeness

>> Shouting

>> Hurtful behaviour

>> Unacceptable risk-taking

>> Bullying

Let's have a go — it won't take long!

Using the categories above, now we're going to sort your teens' behaviour on a chart.

Below is a filled-in version of the behaviour we mentioned above to help you get started. Your list may be quite similar to this one or quite different depending on what you are observing in your teenager. Nevertheless, I would suggest that you and the other adults who live in your house fill in your list together.

Don't worry about the fourth column for now (Big Whats); we'll come to that soon. Do take note of the first three columns.

Example of sorting behaviour chart

Annoying but not serious (ABNS) Ignore these to protect the relationship	Wanted Teach, instil or prompt	Can't-let-that-one-go Hold a tough conversation	'Big Whats' How you describe behaviour you can't let go of
Untidy room

Low-grade rudeness

Being grumpy

Choice of clothes

Pouting

Response of 'Whatever' | A regular contributor to household chores

Eating with the family regularly

Putting dirty clothes in the washing basket

Communicating whereabouts

Being a 'willing' helper | Swearing at others

High-grade rudeness

Shouting

Hurtful behaviour

Unacceptable risk taking

Bullying

Breaking things | Content

Pattern

Relationship |

Over the page is a worksheet you and your partner can complete together. Working together will help you create a united front when dealing with your children. What I want you to do is work out six behaviours that would go in each of the columns, and write these behaviours in the appropriate columns.

Your behaviour-sorting worksheet

ABNS Ignore these to protect the relationship	Wanted Teach or prompt them to do

Can't-let-that-one-go Hold a tough conversation	Big Whats How you describe behaviour you can't let go of
	Content
	Pattern
	Relationship

CPR — a way of *describing* behaviour

Now we come to the fourth column of the behaviour sorting chart; the 'Big Whats' or describing the behaviour. When it comes to behaviour, you're going to need a way of realizing and understanding what's behind it. How we go about explaining the 'Big Whats' becomes an important step in working out how to resolve problems with your teenager. For instance, what may appear to be a problem with your fifteen-year-old daughter repeatedly staying out later than the time you had agreed on might, after some examination, be a problem of poor communication (not telephoning you as she had agreed to when she was running late), broken trust (telling you lies in order to go to parties she knew you would not approve of) or unacceptable risk-taking behaviour (getting lifts with boys who have been drinking).Realizing this, you can work out how to shape the tough conversation you will need to have.

One process to describe behaviour comes out of work done by some World Health Organization experts, Patterson and Grenny, who wrote *Crucial Accountability: Tools for Resolving Violated Expectations, Broken Commitments, and Bad Behavior*, which is about managing workplace disputes. Essentially, they said that if bosses in a workplace are not going to be accusatory or too emotional, they can describe what someone is doing by using the acronym **CPR**: **C**ontent (noting what it looks like and what the facts of it are); **P**attern (noting whether or not it has happened a few times or maybe even more than a few times); and **R**elationships (whether or not what the person is doing is affecting others). Let's take a closer look at these three aspects of behaviour.

We'll return to the CPR method for *describing* unacceptable behaviour in detail in Chapter 7 when we look at how to use a mediation process to hold tough conversations, but what is worth noting here is that we can use ways to describe a problem in terms of these factors.

Some behaviour really needs specialist help

Not all problems can be addressed by us alone. In some instances, you may need to outsource professional help. As a rule of thumb you can generally tell when you need this type of help. If you have seen changes in your teenager's behaviour over the past three months compared to now, or if you notice that their ability to function at school or work is different, then this can be sign of the need for outside help. In fact, one of the criteria psychiatrists and psychologists use to assess mental health is whether there has been a significant change in a young person's ability to function (learn) at school or at work or get along with their peers. While there are symptoms or signs that go with each of these problems, a less direct way of estimating if your young person has problems is to ask the question, 'What has changed in my teen's social or occupational functioning in the past few months?'

>> How are they managing at school?

>> How are they getting along with their friends?

>> Have they lost or gained weight?

>> How are they sleeping?

>> Are they acting differently to how they were three months ago?

In a nutshell, here are ten scenarios when you may need to get help:

1. If your teen wakes up most mornings over a month saying that life is not worth living.

2. If your teen loses a lot of weight quickly or is beginning to look gaunt.

3. If they are using drugs.

4. If they are self-harming.

5. If they are avoiding social situations, wanting to stay home and not go to school or participate in normal activities.

6. If they are displaying persistent low mood.

7. If they have episodes of sudden tearfulness.

8. If they are withdrawing from family relationships.

9. If they have problems getting to sleep, or experience regular wakefulness in the night.

10. If they have loss of appetite.

The best way to assess whether your teenager is having difficulties is to keep the lines of communication open. Really listen, in an engaged, non-judgemental way, without problem solving or advising. If your teenager communicates a worry or concern, try to tune in to them by saying words like, 'You seem really worried about that' or 'I can see that must have been pretty upsetting for you'. Try not to problem solve too early, particularly if they are wound up. If, after really listening, you believe there is a problem that needs addressing, either try to work together to figure out a solution or consider professional help.

In Australia there is an excellent service called Headspace, where trained staff will assess what's going on for your teenager and keep you, their parents, involved in the process. This is a big change from treatment protocols of only a few years back where parents were often left out. For more information, go to http://headspace.org.au.

In Part Two I begin to unpack the best ways you can approach a problem with your teenager. If you are prepared to do some preparation, you will be able to better leverage your efforts. To 'leverage' means to maximize the effects of what you are doing and gain additional power and influence. And that's when using a script can prove very useful.

In essence

» It's important to only have haggles with teens about the serious behaviour that really matters so as not to get into unnecessary power struggles.

» Look for opportunities to thank your teen for their involvement and help with family life.

» Sorting teenagers' behaviour has four main benefits: it stops us reacting by feel, it helps us avoid paying attention to the wrong behaviour, it helps us be more consistent in how to deal with difficult behaviour, and it allows us to be more flexible and less stressed. It also saves us time and energy!

» Sorting behaviour helps you to plan your response. In other words, if you can figure out what behaviour you are seeing, you can choose a better response.

» You can describe unacceptable behaviour by using Content, Pattern and Relationships (CPR). You can use language that is less likely to cause offence while still getting your message across.

PART TWO

USING SCRIPTS SO YOU DON'T FLIP YOUR LID

5

WHY SCRIPTS MATTER

Just prior to the Second World War, pilots began to fly increasingly larger planes. The new planes often had four engines and a lot more complexity than the previous models, and the pilots found themselves suddenly having to keep tabs on many factors at the same time. They just couldn't keep track of all the things that needed their attention, so some fairly large prangs happened! These crashes signalled the need for a better way of managing all the different elements needed to fly these new planes. To solve the problem, a group of test pilots got together and wrote the first 'checklist' — a list of things that a pilot needed to check before taking off.

Checklists enabled the pilots to ensure safety *before* they started engines, *before* attempting take-off, *as they became airborne* and *when landing the plane.* In complex matters, like these, they had to ensure that some things were done before others. The checklists allowed them to manage the stress they experienced in doing their jobs. A checklist is a kind of a script. It alerts the user about what to do first, second, third, etc, and it's the kind of thing you will find handy if you're going to have a tough conversation with your teenager about some serious misbehaviour.

You can walk and chew gum at the same time

Approaching a problem with a teenager can represent a formidable challenge for many parents. Not only do you have to clearly identify and describe the problem to your teenager, you also have to manage their likely reaction to what you may be saying. On top of that you have to manage your own feelings, and not become emotional or heated. To squeeze a bit more out of my flying analogy, imagine that you are flying a plane and you have to manage a flare-out in the left engine. To successfully continue as the pilot in these circumstances, not only do you have to keep flying the plane but you also have to cope with the fire on your wing!

Just as pilots need to follow a set of procedures to put the fire out while they're flying, when you have to have a tough conversation with your teenager you will probably need to manage their flare-ups! In other words, you will have to manage yourself *and* you will have to manage them. Holding a tough conversation with a feisty teenager can be almost as complicated as flying a plane as you will have to keep tabs on a fair few things at once. Having a prepared script will make a big difference.

A script will prescribe what you do at different stages of a tough conversation. You will just do better in solving a problem if you follow a set of steps. This is because you will have pre-planned idea what you are going to say and you won't be as distracted by any flare-ups that eventuate.

This is how pilots train for their jobs. While still on the ground they practise managing typical emergency scenarios — flaps not working, engines flaring out on their wing or wheels not coming down — and they rehearse responding to these situations away from the actual emergency. In other words, in the unlikely event of those things ever happening, they follow the procedures they have previously practised.

While most of us would probably rather have teeth pulled than confront a teenager about an issue such as a breached expectation or broken promise, there is really no other satisfactory way. Of course, I recognize that most teenagers would rather not have a conversation with *you* about a challenging topic. What teenager in their right mind would want to sit down with their oldies and have a discussion about a problem? However, many parents who have used this approach and who have rehearsed what they are going to do report feeling much more empowered by using this type of approach.

Another benefit of using a script to manage a tough conversation is that with repeated use you will find it easier to retrieve information. When pilots practise their flight routines over and over, they end up storing that process differently in their brain. This might sound like a small thing but in fact, by rehearsing something *before it's actually used*, it's more likely that you'll remember it when you are under pressure. This is because practising something over and over saves the information to long-term memory rather than working memory.

It's a bit like the difference between the CPU in a computer and the hard drive. *Working* memory is the CPU and stored memory is the hard drive. Working memory uses lots more energy than stored memory. Working memory is used when we are learning something new, like when we are learning to drive a car and have trouble coordinating the clutch and the accelerator pedals. When you are learning a new skill you're using a lot more mental capacity than if you're using an already practised skill. When we see people doing something complex with ease we say they do it 'effortlessly'. Their lack of apparent effort can be awe-inspiring — but it 'looks' this way simply because they have practised and rehearsed it many times.

Emma Ledden, author of *The Presentation Book*, talks about this phenomenon in relation to public speaking and, more specifically, when people give presentations. It might appear effortless for some people, but the reason it looks like this is because the presenter has prepared. Ledden says:

> The biggest myth on the planet is that you can present well and feel confident with little or no preparation. There is no such thing as a presenter who talks naturally (looks as if they are talking off the cuff and is successful at delivering their message) without proper preparation. It is not possible.

Why am I telling you this?

In the early 1900s scientist Louis Pasteur coined the phrase 'Chance favours the prepared mind'. What he meant by this is that preparation not only improves our ability to do a task but it improves our creativity as well. To be prepared for something means that you can respond flexibly, and, even if the unexpected happens (say, you get interrupted), you can handle it better because your mind has already rehearsed all the possible scenarios.

A script or map of where you are going provides a structure for you to follow. It gives you something to rehearse before any actual events occur so that, if and when they *do* occur, you know what you're going to say.

A big part of your job as the instigator of a tough conversation with a teenager is to keep them 'in' the conversation — and get them to actually stay. I know that some young people are in the habit of avoiding anything that looks like an uncomfortable conversation with their parents. Some 'bolt' at the mere thought of being confronted about their behaviour. They may even refuse to meet, or walk away when their parents want to hold a conversation with them. But you shouldn't let *their* habit put you off, if what they are doing is unacceptable.

In the next few chapters I will show you a range of scripts that cover different scenarios and will help you begin to implement your own preparation to hold similarly tough conversations.

In essence

The skill of holding a tough conversation using a script has a number of payoffs.

- » Scripts allow you to clarify the problem and what you want to say about it.

- » Scripts allow you override emotions to get a job done.

- » Scripts allow you to anticipate how someone might react — and they allow you to sidestep painful points along the way.

- » Scripts provide you with a map of where you'll go in the conversation.

- » Scripts can be prepared in advance of having a tough conversation.

6

PASTA FOR TEENAGERS

People who help others to resolve conflicts use a variety of practical steps. These conflict resolution skills involve using conversation 'rules' to guide what is said during conversations. The rules prescribe a procedure for stating a problem, identifying what you want to change about the problem, and how to manage possible interruptions or objections within the process. Following these rules will help you not only to prepare what you are going to say and *how* you are going to say it, but also to remain calmer and more focused during the discussion.

When it comes to holding a conversation with your teen, writing out what you are going to say beforehand will improve your ability to recall it during the conversation.

When you are resolving a problem with your teenage son or daughter, you'll need to concentrate differently to other times in your communication with them. A good way to think about the type of approach you might have to take is to compare it to the times when you have to fill out a bureaucratic form. For example, when you do this, you often have to provide supporting information such as your driver's licence number or passport details. In other words, you go into business mode. You have to concentrate from the beginning to the end to complete the form. Working out a problem with a teenager can be approached the same way. You just need to focus and be methodical.

In the courses I teach, I say to parents that when they are managing their teenagers' behaviour, they might need to be *temporarily aloof*. In other words, you might also have to behave differently than you do normally. This more serious approach will give the problem you're trying to resolve the gravity it deserves. The other benefit is that if you approach the conversation in a business-like way, you will not be tempted to react. Even if your teenager starts to arc up or dispute you it's best to treat their flare-ups as 'information' rather than personal attacks. If you go into these types of conversations expecting that your teenager will probably be emotional — and you will be able to manage this — you need not let their reactiveness throw you off. If you come at the problem more strategically, you might be able to solve the problem and set the tone for future interactions you'll have with your teenager as well.

As we'll soon see, a small amount of the *right* preparation is a key factor in making tough types of conversations work. Once you have done the preparation a few times, you won't need to prepare as much. As we have discussed, tough conversations are reserved for the big-gish problems that arise from time to time. You won't have to use them that often, but I *do* suggest that in the beginning you get into the habit of thorough preparation.

Comes a time to do something

Let's say something has come up that you *have to* deal with. Your teenager has overstepped a boundary or he has put himself or someone else at risk. Earlier, in Chapter 4, you'll remember that we sorted behaviour into:

»   ABNS

»   Wanted

»   Can't-let-that-one-go.

In this chapter we will look at how to manage the Can't-let-that-one-go types of problems.

ABNS Ignore these to protect the relationship	Wanted Teach or prompt them to do	Can't-let-that-one-go Hold a tough conversation	Big Whats How you describe behaviour you can't let go of
Untidy room	Regular contribution to household chores	Swearing at others	Content
Low-grade rudeness		High-grade rudeness	
Being grumpy	Eating with the family regularly	Shouting	Pattern
Choice of clothes		Hurtful behaviour	
Pouting	Dirty clothes in washing basket	Unacceptable risk	Relationship
'Whatever'			
Choice of music	Communicating her whereabouts	Bullying someone	

As for any conflict resolution method, there are five steps that you can use to deal with problems you encounter with your teenager. These steps are represented by the acronym PASTA. You can see this in the following table. Let's go through each of the steps: Prepare, Appointment, Say, Tame the tiger, Agree.

PASTA

PREPARE
Plan what you're going to say.

APPOINTMENT
Arrange a time and place to meet.

SAY
Say something positive; say what the problem is; say what you want to happen.

TAME THE TIGER
Acknowledge your son or daughter's feelings and needs.

AGREE
Agree on some things that will happen.

P is for Prepare

Prepare by writing down some of your thoughts on paper. Planning what you're going to say will take you about 20 minutes using the worksheets on page 173. Perhaps you could have a look at these pages now, keeping them in mind as we work our way through this process. (However, I suggest that you read through the entire PASTA process before you actually use it in a conversation.) You'll see that the preparation involves being clear about what you want to change, what you're willing to be negotiable about, what your bottom lines are and what will happen if you can't work things out. That's the beauty of having a script to use in these types of situations; it helps you prepare so that you are less likely to be caught out.

A is for Appointment

The purpose of the 'Appointment' part of PASTA is for you to set up a time that avoids having the conversation rushed. Many families tend to deal with problems on the run, whereas they really need to allocate a period of time to work out a problem. Remember you have already decided that the issue is unacceptable, so don't sell yourself or the issue short by handling it on the run. By setting up an appointment with your teenager, you are not only formalizing matters but you are also less likely to see the discussion flare up. Nobody responds well to a challenge 'on the hop'.

In making an appointment you're flagging a *future* meeting you want to hold — that's all. This flagging is important for two reasons: it gives you a strategic advantage — you don't have to have the conversation in a hurry — and secondly, it allows you to determine when and where the conversation will be held.

If you know that your teen is more alert in the morning than in the afternoon, you are better to have the conversation at a time they are likely to be at their best, sunny self. Making an appointment is pretty easy, but you need to do it in such a way that it's not an invitation. In other words, you're not couching it in terms that gives them an 'out'. Now is not the time to debate whether what you want to talk about is a problem or not; the time for *that* has well and truly passed!

Attending the appointment then, is a non-negotiable matter and their participation is merely what you would expect from a person who is becoming more mature. That's what adults do when they have a difference. They sit down and negotiate to see what they can hammer out.

While making the appointment in caveman English may not be advisable — 'You, kitchen, Friday at 4' — you do need to keep your message short and clear.

S is for Say

The 'say' part involves three things:

» Say something nice about them or make a same-page comment.

» Say what the facts of the matter are.

» Say what you want to happen.

Say something nice about them or make a same-page comment

Your opening for this kind of conversation is important if you want to get past first base with your teenager. This is not the time to say things like, 'I suppose you know why we are talking about this,' or to play guessing games with them about why you're having this conversation. Don't launch into a long list of gripes, either

To start on a positive note and in way that they probably *won't* be expecting, say something good about them. If you can't bring yourself to say something nice — because you're too cross for *that* to sound real — you may want to make a comment about being on the 'same page' with them about something. Being on the same page means that you are both aware of something you share in common — and you're happy enough to note it.

For example:

> Let me start by saying that your mum and I are on the 'same page' with you about you going to parties. We know that you will want to go to more parties as you get older, so it's good for us to talk about this now so that our expectations are clear.

Or:

I think we are on the same page with you about you going to parties. That's something that is not in dispute here.

Say what 'the problem' is by using the CPR approach

State as clearly as you can what the facts are by painting a picture by using the CPR (content, pattern, relationship) approach we discussed in Chapter 4. To start with, use words and phrases such as:

Today, I want to talk to you about a problem that Mum and I have seen, and that we'd like to fix if we can. I'd like to begin by telling you what Mum and I have been noticing lately ...

Use words like I have *noticed* and I'm *seeing* and I've *observed*, which will put distance between you and the behaviour. Remember that the main function of the CPR is as a describing tool.

By describing things in this way, you are less likely to fall into the trap of blaming your teen (which will make them defensive). You can then say, 'This is not the first time we have had to talk about this' (noting the pattern) and mention how this problem affects you or others.

Say what you want from them

At some point in the conversation, you'll have to tell your teen what you want to happen. In doing this, you will have had a chance to consider what you are asking of them. You don't want to make a rod for your own back by insisting on things that ultimately you can't enforce. By writing out what you want beforehand, you're less likely to be unrealistic in your demands. Requiring your teenager to call you every hour on the hour while they're at a party with their friends is probably not only unreasonable but it's also unlikely to work. That would be a frustrating requirement for everyone.

For example:

> So, given all of that [what you have just explained to them] here is what I want to happen in the future: Firstly, secondly, thirdly ...

T is for Tame the tiger

As you are moving through the 'say' parts of PASTA, chances are that your teenagers will interrupt you. They may want to dispute your version of events or minimize what you're saying. Taming the tiger is the part of PASTA where you get to deal with interruptions. When it comes to dealing with a challenging teenager, it is to be expected that they will become defensive. If you expect this, you won't be as stumped or offended. Remember, while *you* may be incredibly interested in wanting to solve a problem, they won't be. Chances are that they will want you out of their space. Chances are also that they will obstruct you in your effort to discuss a problem.

If your teen becomes upset or angry, it may be time to 'down tools' on the 'Say' part and reset the conversation. You can do this by listening for the emotion in their presentation to you — paying attention to their frustration, anger or dismay, then treating those feelings (even if they're partly directed at you) as information or data. That information can be filed or dealt with, but not ignored. It doesn't require you to launch a full-scale counter-attack. If you don't see it as an attack (but data), you can then make a choice to engage with them in a different way. You can *acknowledge* what they are feeling.

I know from my own professional experience that this strategy of momentarily listening works. In my work in the family court with couples in dispute over child custody, I saw many people who were facing some very stressful times. When people became upset with their partner or about the unfairness of their situation, I knew it was important to hear what they had to say, before trying to move on and focus on solving their particular problem. You might have to engage in an emotional process (listening) before you can move on to the problem-solving process (where you are trying to build bridges to seek an agreement).

What you can expect when you challenge behaviour

Teenagers are still learning the emotional ropes and how to tussle with strong feelings. Sometimes their pre-frontal ability to coordinate a number of things simultaneously — identifying emotions in their bodies, assessing the gravity of the situation and working how to hold it all together — is impaired or not working smoothly. Teenagers are also more likely than adults to misread the emotions of others, so they may mistakenly think a parent is angry even when they are not. Or, alternatively, some have developed bad behaviour over a long period of time. Either way it's worth listening to see if you can settle them down before moving on with the conversation.

Under psychiatrist Scott Peck's model we spoke about earlier in Chapter 1, with greater maturity comes greater ability to coordinate all these factors described above and to get things in proportion. So, if you bring up something that they don't want to discuss, something that challenges their worldview, don't be surprised if they react poorly. Depending on the maturity of your teenager, that kind of response is to be expected. Here is a list of some typical reactions:

When challenged, teens might:

» minimize the effects of their actions on others

» become defensive and withdrawn

» arc up and use anger to divert the discussion

» dispute your version of events

» project blame on to others

» accuse you of making a big deal out of nothing

» say it has nothing to do with you

» insult you.

Each of these kinds of outbursts is an outward expression of some level of frustration. For many parents the deluge of innuendo or insult can be relentless. The barrage of barbs — aimed at getting you to back off — can be intimidating and hurtful. In response to these objections, you may be tempted to do some of the following:

» Respond defensively with the 'I'm in charge here' routine and say, 'You can't talk to me like that. How dare you be so rude?'

» Argue with them about how you are right and they are wrong.

» Give them an uncalled for insight transplant: 'You know when I was your age, I ...'

However, none of these retorts is productive in fixing the problem at hand. Remember, you're the adult here. You can get offended for sure, but your job is not to get carried away by your emotions.

To tame a tiger is to defuse emotional reactions by attempting to engage with your teenager's emotions. By being organized and working on the basis that your teen actually has *some* ability to exert self-control, you can help them apply the brakes to their runaway emotions.

Sometimes when teenagers get het up, you can actually help them calm down by naming what's going on. Remember that 'acknowledging' what they're feeling is not 'agreeing' with what they're saying. It's just noting what you see. If your teen gets upset while you are talking, step back in your mind from what you are saying to acknowledge what they are experiencing. By listening like this, even for a short time, your teen will feel heard and there's more of a chance they'll stick around for the rest of the conversation. Remember three things:

1. You can afford to go with their emotion for a moment during the 'say' part of PASTA because you're prepared. You know what you're going to say and you'll be able to pick up the thread of the conversation where you left off. So, it doesn't matter if it takes a minute or two longer while you hear them out.

2. You can generally resolve their frustrations by making three, four or five clear statements about their emotional state. (I'll show you how to do this shortly.)

3. By acknowledging the emotional elements in your teenager's response you are also helping *them* better understand their own emotional terrain.

You can put what *you* want to say 'on hold' to restore their feelings of safety, before returning to the topic by saying something like, 'I can see that what I am saying is really annoying for you. I know that you generally try to drive safely. I want to find a way for us both to be happy with your driving but I am hearing how frustrating talking about this is for you.'

The trick here is to momentarily step out of the 'say' part of the conversation by bookmarking where you are up to and then turning your attention to what they may be experiencing. As I say, up to four or five tuning-in statements is usually enough, after which you will come to a natural lull.

Then you can return to where you left off. The lull in the conversation you will probably arrive at is not unlike what we talked about earlier, where a teenager might scrunch up their face up as if to maintain control. By this time, they've run out of puff, emotionally. In the case studies coming up in Chapter 8 you will see how this works.

In the end, of course, even this strategy may not work but remember you always have an escape route; you can always stop the conversation and walk away. You don't have to allow yourself to be abused by your teen. (If this is a continual problem, then maybe it's time to get some professional help. Doing so, by the way, does not mean that you have done a poor job or that your son or daughter is a lost cause. Sometimes troubling patterns in families can be hard to break.)

Affect clusters are a device for identifying emotions

As we have discussed, a key component of taming your teenager's interruptions is being able to *imagine* how they will react as you progress through the PASTA process but particularly in the 'say' part. Because you have already worked out what you are going to say by the time you hold the conversation with them, you can afford to be taken off track if they interrupt you. If they jump at you (figuratively speaking), you can take stock by momentarily focusing on their feelings. This strategy is useful in at least two ways: first, you're more likely to keep them in the conversation than if you just tell them to not interrupt you, and second, you will be able to pursue what you want to say after you have drained the emotion out of the charged situation.

When you are considering your teenager's frustration with the process or with you, during a tough conversation, that frustration usually stems from a number of emotions and can be described from a number of angles.

I call this collection of feelings an 'affect cluster'. A neat way to visualize an affect cluster is by using the image of a three-dimensional diamond.

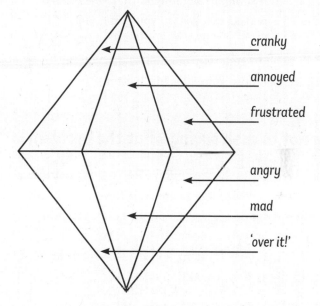

But by paying attention to your teenager's affect cluster you can do a lot to help them to 'hang in there' in the middle of a tough conversation. Paying attention to more than one emotion also helps defuse the situation emotionally, as generally there is more than one emotion in play at any given time.

Here are two main taming strategies you can use if they become upset:

1. **Reflective statements,** where you name the emotions that the other person is feeling. For example:

    > I can see that you are really frustrated that Mum and I want to bring this issue up with you. I suppose in your mind we are making a bigger deal out of this than is necessary.

2. **Contrast statements,** which help clarify your
statements. For example:

> I am not saying that you can't go to the
> party; I am saying that we need to work
> out some arrangements that will reduce
> any risks involved in you going out.

(These two are generally enough to get you out of trouble, but
there are five more strategies in Chapter 9.)

Try not to rush *saying* what the problem is

Once you get to the 'say' part of PASTA, try not to rush
when stating 'what' the problem is to your teen. You're not
pulling them up for a just a minor issue. You don't have to
apologize or feel sorry that they may get upset. If you have
raised an issue with them, you've already worked out that
you're doing it for a good reason.

In the 'say' part of PASTA you're describing what you're
seeing, and you're also telling them how what they're doing
is affecting others. Again, you're not expecting them to
agree with you. By describing the content, its pattern and
the effects of the problem, you are making the invisible
visible — and for this you need to take your time. I have
noticed that even among the professionals I teach there is
a tendency to rush the middle part of 'say'. I think people
feel that the content part of 'say' is secondary to the really
important part of 'say' which is the say-what-you-want
part. In my opinion, it isn't.

So why go through the CPR process with them? Why not
just cut to the chase and tell them what you want?

Using CPR helps lay out your concerns logically and one by one. By describing what your teen is doing, you are providing them with a view of things they may not have considered. They won't get that if you rush it. Your view, in fact, is a considered understanding — one on which you have spent some time . By sufficiently outlining what you see as the problem, you're giving your teen your *considered* response. You should lead them through the logical sequence of your CPR view: how their actions result in consequences and how their actions are contrary to what your family thinks are important. These may be uncomfortable 'facts', but all of us have to struggle with (and interpret) uncomfortable facts. By 'framing' things like this you're describing how their actions are affecting others and the consequences that may be invisible to them. Only then might they see what their behaviour looks like, and how serious it is. Only then will they fully appreciate how their actions are affecting others. Our job in parenting teens is not only to expect better behaviour and help them with their emotions; it is also to help them see the bigger picture, which is something that only you, with your fully functioning mind, can see.

Maintain a certain tone

If you are to have any chance of sounding real, not only is it important to choose words that reflect what your teenager is feeling but also that you look somewhat earnest and that the sound of your voice reflects the gravity of *their* emotion. So, when you are using reflective statements it's important not to sound patronizing or like 'the counsellor'. Nothing will put your teenager off more than if you sound like you are doing some kind of therapy number on them.

In music, the word discordant means a lack of harmony between two notes. The same applies here. When you are reflecting back to your teenager what you notice — that they are angry or frustrated — it's really important to put some of the same emotion in *your* voice. So, if they are feeling angry, you need to look and sound a bit annoyed. This is called resonance, when someone is in that moment with you. This means not just hearing them, but it is also nearly matching the strength of that emotion. It's the difference between sounding patronizing and 'like the counsellor' and really connecting with what they are experiencing.

So, for example, if they are at an eight out of ten level of anger, you will need to use at least a six out of ten level of tone. Then the next time you respond at a five, and then a three. You don't need to sound angry but you do need to reflect their emotion with a tone that nearly matches theirs.

Here are a few example sentences you might say, with a bit of 'gravel' and earnestness in your voice:

> 'I can really hear how much this means to you.'

> 'It looks incredibly frustrating for you to hang in here and talk about this.'

> 'I can see how much this means to you.'

Pursue the lull

Managing the process of keeping your teen 'in the conversation' is also about your timing and the ability to know when to say things and, also, when *not* to. You can drain the emotion out of many a situation by reflecting on and acknowledging what the other person is experiencing,

What will eventually happen is that you will reach a point where there is nowhere to go. You'll most likely come to a natural lull or pause in the conversation. Then the best thing you can do at this point is shoosh.

This lull in the conversation is a space where your teen will feel acknowledged and where they will be trying to get a grip on their emotions. You need not jump in to protect them from this discomfort. Your teen may be grimacing or screwing up their face, but this is to be expected as they make sense of things. It is very common when people don't say something for us to want to jump in to fill the void, but at this point it is better not to.

If you do your job properly by hearing how it is for them three, four or five times, they will just run out of puff, emotionally. If you fill the void with another comment, while they are doing this, you are interrupting a mental process where they are pulling themselves together. Remember what Siegel said earlier? 'If a parent cannot tolerate a child's being upset, it is very difficult for the child to regulate her emotions.' So 'mind the gap' and don't be tempted to use words like 'but' or 'however', which are words that will take them back into their logical part of their brain and where they will be tempted to restart the argument with you again.

So, if you *stage* a PASTA conversation, you can achieve the following:

- » Solve the problem at hand.
- » Help your teenager to identify, track and manage their feelings so they can self-manage.
- » Teach your teen how people solve problems and negotiate.

Navigating PASTA is like sailing a boat

Following a script like PASTA enables you to get from point A (the beginning) to point B (a solution) and deal with interruptions as they happen. You have your script (PASTA) with your purpose and goals clarified but your teen will have their agenda too — to dispute and minimize the issue in order to get their own way.

During your conversation, you'll spend most of your time in the 'say' section but an analogy that works here is that it's like sailing a boat that needs to navigate to get from one point to another and the prevailing conditions mean you might have to change direction occasionally. In other words, you're working your way towards your objective and you can afford to go slightly off-course to eventually get to the place you want to go.

In order for you to keep moving forward, you're going to have to acknowledge what your adolescent is saying. Once you have done that, however, it's time to get back to where you left off in your process. This stopping is called bookmarking. Your bookmark is where you've got to in the PASTA process and you then return to that place to continue on with the process. Like a sailing boat has to momentarily shift direction to cater for the prevailing conditions, you'll need to help your teen to settle before continuing on with your script.

I am not suggesting that you should tolerate all manner of behaviour that might get heaped on you during this time. I am saying though that they may need your help to contain themselves or to get a grip. And while you shouldn't ignore their interjections, you need to be guided more by your PASTA script than by their reactions. 'Taming the tiger' is a set of strategies that will help you harness big-ish emotions that we will see used in the case studies coming up in Chapter 8. These tactics will help you deal with strong emotion, without panicking.

A is for Agree

The final part of PASTA is where *you* sum up your understanding of what you are agreeing about and how your teen will meet certain agreed upon behaviours within a certain time frame. (If you can sell this to them by outlining what's in it for them, then even better.) For example, you tell them what you have agreed about.

'Okay, so what we have agreed upon is:

» I will keep my comments about your driving to an absolute minimum when we go for driving lessons; this will mean we won't be talking as much.

» I will try extra hard to let you know when you are doing well.

» You've agreed to follow my instructions when I see something potentially dangerous happening.'

Ending with a mutual agreement is an important part of summing up and finalizing the conversation. It leaves both you and your teen with a clear understanding of what is expected.

In the last two chapters we have seen how a set of instructions — a script — can help you to initiate and prepare for difficult conversations. In the next chapter, we look at ways in which you can handle yourself under pressure during a tough conversation.

In essence

» Scripts help parents describe what they want to talk to their teenager about.

» PASTA provides parents with a sequence of steps aimed at solving a problem.

» PASTA give parents a series of statements they can make to help their teenager calm down.

» PASTA helps demonstrate a process for teenagers that shows them how 'mature' people negotiate.

» PASTA gives young people a safe place to express their frustrations, but is also a process where they can be taught to exert self-control.

7

HOLDING YOUR NERVE

As a psychologist, I have had to write many child welfare reports which were held accountable under cross-examination in court. Unless I had done the interviews properly and prepared the report well — that is, logically and coherently — I could expect to be duly trounced by a ravenous barrister and, sometimes, even a judge. In these situations thinking on my feet, under pressure, became essential.

This kind of thinking is a bit different from what happens in a normal conversation, because the court is testing the evidence. This is how adversarial courts work. The barrister is assessing the logic of my report. As the client's advocate the barrister is most interested in either supporting my views (if the report is in the client's favour) or throwing rocks at them (if the report goes against the client). In defending a position — a bit like how a cricketer defends his stumps — I had to get better at holding my nerve and thinking under pressure. In fact, I learnt a lot from doing this over and over.

My dealings with the law have taught me three things:

1. Preparation is a key to being cross-examined.

2. Don't react immediately — take the time to think before replying.

3. The more preparation I had done the better I performed.

What I also learnt from appearing in court was that nine times out of ten, I was nearly always more across the case than the barrister. Most barristers only had time to read my report the morning of the court appearance, whereas I had taken a few weeks to collect all the information, write up the report and give some thought to questions I might be asked. Being better prepared than the barristers meant that I was able to handle even the curliest of crosses. In order to have a successful tough conversation with your teen, you might want to think about preparing as though you will be facing a barrister ... and in many ways you may feel you are being cross-examined.

'How is football like a conversation with a teen?'

Let me tell you a rugby story to show you what I mean by the ability of adults to hold it together under pressure. My story demonstrates how an adult is able to wrestle with competing urges and keep control of their emotions. This is very much like a situation you might find yourself in when holding a tough conversation with a teen.

Imagine Australia is playing New Zealand in a game of rugby. There's a roaring crowd; TV commentators are up in the box; and New Zealand has drawn a scrum as a result of knock on from an Australian player. It's close to fulltime and Australia is in front by a whisker. New Zealand is close to the Australian line. The referee sets the scrum but it buckles upwards and very quickly a New Zealand player jabs a punch, hitting his opposite number. The Aussie player hits back and a fracas breaks out. Punches fly left and right and it would appear that every player is involved in the ensuing skirmish. As the dust settles, the linesman accuses the Aussie player of starting the fight. The Australian is called before the referee. His body language belies his emotional state. He is seething mad. After all, he didn't throw the first punch.

Inside his head, the player's brain is going a thousand miles an hour. One part of his brain, often referred to as 'the old brain', is responsible for immediate and instinctive responses and it is demanding that he, 'Hit the ref. Give the ref a spray. Lose it!' The front part of his brain, his new brain, is desperately clinging onto some form of self-control. This part of his mind is saying, 'Don't hit the ref ... I'll be suspended if I touch him ... I'll be sent off, better hold it together.'

This process of moving between these two parts of his brain — I call it toggling — is an attempt to 'hold' onto, or inhibit, an emotional reaction to what has occurred. No doubt the player was wrestling with some very strong emotions, but he was able to remonstrate with himself to hold it together.

You too can do this if you feel provoked by your teenager. By keeping your wits about you, you can wrestle with your emotional reactions and keep what you want to do or say in your mind's eye. Believe it or not, it is something you can do — just as I learnt to do in the witness box. Like the footballer, you can quickly wrestle with your thoughts of retaliation by holding your nerve. Holding your nerve is as much about you having alternatives in your mind's eye as it is in keeping yourself from flipping your lid. That's where preparing a PASTA script can be invaluable.)

So, there are two parts to responding well when your teenager arcs up: not taking their reaction personally; and having something at hand to respond with. Understanding this is vital, because if you can't to do the first part well, you're unlikely to know how to do the second part well. The trick here is to not let your teen's emotions throw you off. This is often easier said than done, I know. But if you take the right attitude into the conversation, you can make adjustments here and there before getting back on track. Sure, you could get uppity back at them but that would get in the way of fulfilling the purpose of your conversation, which is, above all, to solve a problem and to teach them how to negotiate.

The right attitude

As we have discussed previously, if you go into these types of conversations in a business-like mode you'll be able to cope with interruptions and distractions a lot better. You will also need to put aside any need you might have to want to be 'liked'. I think many parents fear that if they challenge their teen's behaviour they will be perceived as 'uncool'. I appreciate that this can be a difficult issue. No-one likes saying no and sometimes it takes a great deal of courage to hold a firm line about something. This is the part where I ask you to develop a thick skin.

The one thing I do know, though, is that the vast majority of teenagers share a wonderful thing with their parents called attachment. Them being attached to you and you to them means that you have credits in a relationship bank account and you can afford to make withdrawals from that account from time to time. The very first thing you need to remind yourself in order to hold your nerve is that there's this invisible umbilical cord that connects you and them — and it's not going to break as the result of the odd argument.

But knowing this, and not being afraid, is about more than just reassuring yourself; it's also about not getting spooked when you don't need to. If your teen pushes back, gets angry or even insults you, it's about you knowing what you can do to handle this.

Approach any problem like it's a dispute with a neighbour

If you have to hold a tough conversation with your teenager, you will need to approach it with a certain persona — one where your feathers are not easily ruffled. It may sound a bit odd, but I want to ask you to consider the idea that if you are going to hold a difficult conversation with a poorly behaved teenager, approach it like you would if you were solving a problem with *a neighbour*. Just run with me on this for a moment!

For example, say one of your neighbours played their music too loud or parked in your car spot, more than likely you'd first approach them calmly. Remember what Peck said: it's about knowing when to become strident or take a stand that reflects a person's maturity. You see, if there was a problem with your neighbour I suspect that, in the first instance, you probably wouldn't spit the dummy at them straight away. Well, I don't know *you* personally — maybe you would! But I suspect that you would realize that you're going to have to live next door to your neighbour for the foreseeable future, and you'd try to use common sense to solve the problem. In other words, you wouldn't come at them all guns blazing. This is also the best approach when sorting out things with your teenager. Approach it matter-of-factly and don't get into the habit of doing a Gordon Ramsay on them. As you know, when neighbours start yelling at each other the situation almost always never improves and the chances of the problem being solved are drastically reduced. It is the same when holding tough conversations with your teen.

In your case your dispute with your teenager — and let's face it, it *is* a dispute — need not be a mess. But, unless at least one of you goes into a tough conversation with the right attitude, it will be. Dana Caspersen, the author of *Changing the Conversation*, says, 'We can change the nature of the conversation we are part of, even if others continue with an attack/counterattack methodology.' She goes on to say, 'Resisting the urge to attack does not mean that we leave ourselves with no protection and no power. It means that we can turn the focus of the conversation away from the distraction of attack and towards what is important on a deeper level.' In other words, you can temporarily take your emotions out of the equation, if you know what your ultimate goal is.

Control the controllables

After I published my first book, *Talk Less Listen More*, which is about managing behaviour problems in children, I had to do some radio and TV interviews. A radio broadcaster friend of mine told me that I would do better as an interviewee if I prepared a song sheet with five points that I wanted to talk about. In media interviews, the term song sheet is used to describe the main points you want to speak about when you're on air. You see, even though I couldn't guess what the interviewer would ask me, it didn't mean I couldn't prepare. My friend told me that there are some questions you can predict like, 'Why did you write this book?' or 'What are your top three tips for parents?' But what I also found is that if I wrote down five points I wanted to talk about, there was usually a chance to mention them somewhere in the interview. By doing some easy preparation I was not only able to tell my story well; I was also able to communicate to the listener the points I wanted to discuss.

In sports psychology, coaches urge players to 'control the controllables'. This is when you take care of the things that you can control. Manchester United's football coach Sir Alex Ferguson inspired this approach in his players. They could not control the crowd noise and they could not control the referee's decisions but they could control their preparation for the match and their thoughts about the game.

When I have treated people who have been involved in a trauma following an accident or if they had been a victim of crime, they often found themselves getting upset when others asked after their wellbeing. The people who asked how they were doing were not intentionally upsetting my clients, but sometimes even slightly recalling a trauma brought up raw emotions. This brought a feeling of being out of control, particularly when out in public. Sometimes my clients felt like they couldn't even walk down a street without someone potentially asking them about their wellbeing.

Although they couldn't control what other people said to them, my clients could control their reaction to it. I gave them some lines they could use so that they didn't get so upset and that helped them to not be rude when someone genuinely inquired after their wellbeing. My clients would say something like, 'Thank you for asking me about how I am going. It's been hard, but I think I'm getting a bit better each day. Now, how are you?' This response was enough to acknowledge the other person's perfectly reasonable wish to be caring, but not so much that it led them to become upset. My clients memorized it and practised it so that they could pull out a pre-planned response, without becoming upset. They were controlling what they could control.

Visualize yourself coping in a conversation with your teenager

Having a plan is one thing, but it is no substitute for real-match experience. However, you can *imagine* how you are going to react and doing this is an important part in holding your nerve throughout a tough conversation with your teenager. In other words, this is when you picture yourself in a tough conversation and imagining how you'll react.

For example:

» Imagine where you are going to be sitting when you're having the conversation. In fact, I suggest that you actually sit there and imagine starting the conversation.

» Think how your teenager might be, what they'll look like (probably grumpy) and how you'll respond if they get uppity with you.

» Imagine yourself staying calm but firm and insisting on what you need while also giving ground where you need to.

» Notice any negative or angry reactions you might be feeling and think about how you would restrain these.

» Visualize yourself responding if they get upset.

Performance coaches ask their players to do this kind of thing all the time. They tell athletes to imagine kicking that goal into the back of the net or clearing the high jump bar. I suggest you do the same if you are going to have a tough conversation with your teenager. Just a little bit of written preparation and some visualizing can go a long way towards helping you remain composed.

To sum up, here are the three controllables you can focus on when you are going to hold a tough conversation.

1. **You can control the attitude *you* take into the conversation**. You can make a decision to go into the situation with courage and firmness. You don't need to fight.

2. **You can control the script you'll write and say,** which will enable you to be well prepared to solve the problem. If your teenager gets upset, you can use tame the tiger lines to get the conversation back on track.

3. **You can control what you imagine** and how you *see* yourself coping in the conversation — even before you have it. In other words, you can visualize success!

Controllables	Uncontrollables
The attitude you take into the conversation	Your teenager's attitude or sense of entitlement
Your written script	The topic
What you visualize yourself doing	Your teenager's reactions or their friends' views

Some other points to remember:

» Decide that you will not lose your temper or retaliate. If it goes badly just *stop* the conversation.

» Don't blame your teenager for attempting to upset you — just expect it, and manage it.

» Relax, and let go of the idea that you have to get it exactly right.

Don't work out problems when you're tired or irritated

We all know that we are less patient when we're tired. So, if you're tired, it's probably not the best time to work on a teenager's misbehaviour.

If *you* are tired and irritable when you try to approach them about what they are doing, there's a high likelihood that you'll end up yelling at them or it will morph into a runaway argument. While it's tempting to launch into a 'rocket attack' the moment you find out that something bad has happened, it's probably wiser to hold off and work out a plan. I know it can be tempting to have it out with them at 3 am when they have finally come home or when you've just found out from your sister that your daughter has posted something unseemly on Facebook. But wherever possible, don't react immediately, unless it has something to do with their safety.

As far as your teenager is concerned, don't engage in a tough conversation when *they* are also tired or preoccupied. If you don't want to get unnecessary blow back stemming from *their* tiredness or stress, you'll need to pick your moment to challenge them.

In the next chapter, I will show you three conversations a case study family, the Coopers, have used to resolve unacceptable behaviour with their teenagers. The actual content of the problem doesn't matter. As I said earlier, by using the PASTA process you will develop the skills for handling all types of conversation topics. What you'll see in the next chapter is the Coopers applying the same skills across three different situations. You will be able to use these same skills to resolve almost any problem you will encounter.

In essence

- » We can control our emotional responses and we should help our kids to learn to do the same.

- » We have the ability to step back from the emotion a teen's behaviour might trigger and view the situation more objectively.

- » Avoid taking action when you are angry, upset or frustrated by your teen's behaviour. Wait until you have cooled down. Try to look at the problem more systematically.

- » There are at least three things you can control: your attitude, your preparation and how you visualize yourself coping during a tough conversation.

- » Preparation is the key to thinking on your feet.

- » You can tolerate a little rudeness up to a point.

- » Give yourself the best chance of succeeding by picking the right moment to have a conversation, not when you or your teen is tired or angry.

PART THREE

CASE STUDIES AND WORKSHEETS TO USE AT HOME

8

THREE SERVES OF PASTA

The Coopers

To help us get started with the PASTA process we're going to look at a family with three teenagers. The Coopers have dealt with some pretty common problems while bringing up their three teenagers, such as the over-use of technology, not getting enough sleep, ignoring curfews and risk-taking behaviour. In this chapter, we're going to look at how the Coopers overcame these problems and how they resolved the issues satisfactorily through engaging in some tough conversation with their three teenage children.

Before we get started though, I think it's timely to revisit a few things in a summary form. Then we'll get straight into the case studies.

To recap:

» Mums and dads with their fully mature minds are in a much better position to work out what behaviour crosses the line than are teenagers. There will be plenty of room for teenagers to explore their surroundings, seek novelty and push boundaries, but a major job of parents is one of appropriate containment. It is not about spoiling their fun — although some displeasure may happen along the way.

» All things being equal, you won't have to intervene as much in your teenagers' lives the older they get. If you've put some good guardrails in place you can reasonably expect that they will move through their teenage years without too many disruptions to their normal development.

» Assuming they are sleeping well and not using drugs or alcohol, or too much aggro-inducing technology, we can also assume that most teens are capable of premeditation, which is a necessary condition for being able to hesitate long enough to make good decisions. We can reasonably expect their ability to exert self-control will kick in most of the time.

» Finally, to get the best out of tough conversations, you'll need to approach them like you're solving a problem with a neighbour, calmly and matter-of-factly.

Okay, with those little reminders place, here we go.

Jane Cooper is a 40-year-old mum who works part-time at the local school. Andrew is a 42-year-old baggage handler at the nearby airport and works shift work. Their three teenagers are thirteen-year-old Tom, fifteen-year-old Emma, and Seb, who is seventeen years old.

Using the problems outlined below, I want to show you how our host family, the Coopers, have approached issues in their family using the PASTA process. You will see how the Coopers prepared themselves by writing out a script and how they managed their children's frustration.

In other words, I will show you how they were successful at being both the mediator *and* the parent. Not quite the juggling act it looks, but it is made easier when I highlight some key strategies to help you stay on track. In each of these cases, the Coopers have decided that what each of their children is doing is unacceptable and they need to have a tough conversation with them.

The problems

Tom has been irritable and short-tempered with everyone at home over the past two months. Lately, Jane has heard Tom talking to his friends late at night in his bedroom and she's recently found him playing a violent multi-player video game at 1 am on a school night when she thought he was asleep. His teachers have reported that his schoolwork has deteriorated and his parents are not happy that he has been falling asleep at odd times during the day. He has been checked by their GP and he doesn't have any illnesses as far as they know, so they have ruled that out. Normally Jane is happy to let Tom talk to his friends on Facebook and play video games but there are limits and they have let Tom's behaviour go on too long. It's time for a talk.

Emma has been coming home late from parties. In the past few months the problem of Emma getting home later than the agreed time has been very worrying for both her parents. When she is out Emma has not been answering her mobile, so she has been hard to communicate with. She has been secretive about where she is going and argumentative much of the time. Now Emma wants to go to a party that all her friends are going to. Her parents don't want a repeat of previous party problems, so they're going to have a conversation with Emma to sort some things out.

Seb is on his L-plates. He has accrued 60 hours of driving practice but has become increasingly cocky and has been taking big risks while at the wheel. Driving with his father the other day, he ignored an instruction to slow down and nearly hit a four-year-old girl who was with her mother on the side of the road. His parents have decided that they cannot take Seb for future driving lessons without first talking to him about the incident and getting some undertakings from him about his behaviour. After all, if this behaviour goes unchecked, next time he might kill someone.

Case study 1: Tom the late-night gamer

As we have read, the Coopers' thirteen-year-old son Tom has been irritable and short-tempered with everyone at home over the past two months.

When confronted about his behaviour Tom is likely to feel the following:

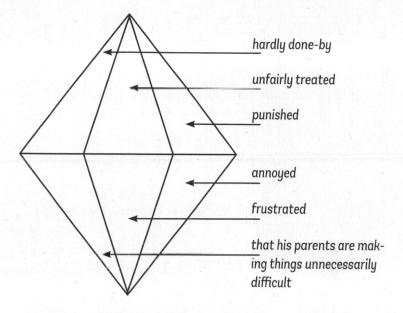

hardly done-by

unfairly treated

punished

annoyed

frustrated

that his parents are making things unnecessarily difficult

These are all fairly normal reactions from a boy of Tom's age who is being confronted about his behaviour. He is not a kid with delinquency problems but, like anybody, he's going to find it tough to contain all his emotions when someone challenges his assumption that he can do what he wants. Tom is likely to feel that his parents are picking on him, that they are being too harsh, and that they are trying to punish him. Tom's script in the tough conversation will be very different to that of his parents.

Take 1: The train wreck

A few weeks back Tom's dad Andrew made a failed attempt at talking with Tom about his staying up too late. This is how that conversation went down. Andrew caught Tom on his way out the door.

Andrew: Hey Tommo, before you go, I've been telling you for weeks that I don't want you using your phone after lights are out.

Tom:	What! What is the matter with you?!
Andrew:	I want you to just do as I say, that's what the matter is.
Tom:	Yeah, sure. [slinking away, trying to avoid his dad]
Andrew:	Tom, I mean it. It's lights out at 9.30 and I want the phone left in the kitchen overnight from now on.
Tom:	No way! What kind of *place* are you running here?
Andrew:	My kind of place.
Tom:	This is fucked!
Andrew:	Listen buster, Mum and I make the rules around here, not you!
Tom:	No other kid has to put up with this rubbish. Josh's parents let him have his phone all the time.
Andrew:	Well, guess what, pal? We're not Josh's parents, we're yours — so shape up.
Tom:	[Mumbling] You're a pathetic joke!

Here you can see Andrew made some classic mistakes: he attempted to talk with Tom while he was rushing out the door. As a result Tom became rude and stormed off. This very common scenario happens many times in households all across the country every day. It's what comes with rushing things and not giving matters the attention they need. In this conversation nothing was resolved and Tom was furious about his dad's request.

Take 2: A better run through

Now we will assume that Jane and Andrew have learnt how to use the PASTA script. The first thing they need to do is prepare what they are going to say. They need to clarify in their minds what their bottom lines are, what they're willing to negotiate about and what will happen if it all fails — their stop-gap measure.

P is for Prepare

Here's how the preparation conversation goes:

Jane: I can't believe that Tom was up again the other night playing that multiplayer game at two in the morning. It was a school night! What's going on with him? He knows better than that.

Andrew: Sometimes he's been up doing the phone thing as well. He's been well and truly pushing the boundaries with the screen stuff lately.

Jane: I don't know … at one level, it's what a lot of boys his age are doing, but he's been an irritable little bugger lately. I reckon half of it's because he hasn't been sleeping properly.

Andrew: I think we should have a talk with him. What do you say we organize to meet with him on Saturday? How about ten o'clock or so?

Jane: Good idea.

Andrew: Who's going to tell him?

Jane:	I will. I'll line him up before I go to work in the morning.
Andrew:	Maybe we can have a go at a PASTA script together? I'll get some ideas down on paper.
Jane:	Yeah, good idea. I think we need to show him we're united on this.

The Coopers are off to a good start. They fill out their preparation worksheets. In the next chapter we'll see how the Coopers put their script together. Let's get straight into the action first and see where the conversation goes.

A is for Appointment

Jane nominated herself to organize the appointment. She is calm as she approaches Tom, who's having his cereal. She knows what she's going to say and she has thought about what she has to do if Tom interrupts her.

Jane:	So, Tom, what have you got on at school today?
Tom:	Mmm, it's Soph's birthday so they're doing a cake thing.
Jane:	Well, wish her a happy birthday from me. Hey, before I go to work, I want to make a time to talk about the internet and a few things that have been happening lately.
Tom:	[Immediately defensive] What? Why do we have to do that? Why do we have to talk about it?
Jane:	[Focused, not taking the bait, but finishing what she wants to say] Tom, now's not a good time to discuss this as I have to get to

work. But your dad and I want to talk with you about some things we've been meaning to sort out for a while. So, I'd really like you to be part of that conversation. You're a teenager now and it'll be good for you to negotiate some things with us. We can have some cake in the lounge room on Saturday at ten o'clock. Okay?

Tom: [Grimacing, rolling his eyes] What's there to sort out?

Jane: [Speaking calmly, again she's not thrown by Tom's reaction] We'll talk at ten on Saturday, Tom.

Tom: Not ten. Joe and I are skating on Saturday.

Jane: Well, twelve o'clock. You should be home by then.

Tom: [Grumbling, reluctant] But Mum, I don't get it. Why do we have to do this?

Jane: [Ignoring Tom's pleading] Why don't you have a think about what you want to say? We'll talk about it on Saturday at about twelve, with some cake.

Jane does well. She doesn't try to have the conversation there and then with Tom. She tells Tom *what* she wants to discuss with him, and *where* and *when* it will happen. She stays calm throughout. A good start is made.

S is for Say something affirming

It's twelve o'clock on Saturday at the Cooper residence. Jane, Andrew and Tom gather in the lounge room as arranged.

Andrew: [Knowing he has to begin the conversation positively] You right, Tom? Mum and I would like to start, if you're ready. Good on you, mate.

Tom: Do we have to do this? What's the big deal?

Andrew: Yes, mate, we have to. Look, the first thing I want say is that we think you're mostly doing really well at the moment. We like that you are going out and playing sport, and it's great that you're so interested in motorbikes.

Tom: [Sighing, groaning] How long's this going to take? I've got stuff to do, y'know, like homework and …

Andrew: [Making a statement of common ground] You're a great boy, Tom. If we can agree about some things we won't have to hassle you. I'm sure you don't want us nagging you about stuff all the time, so I'm hoping we can work out an agreement between us. That way we can put this behind us and move on.

Tom: [Sniping, attacking] You just want to control me all the time. Why can't I live my own life?

Andrew: [Staying focused and in control, not taking the bait] Well, I guess you won't want us being in charge forever, but given that you are thirteen, we still have a say for the moment.

Tom: [Fuming at having to go through this humiliating conversation]

Andrew's off to a good start here. He's said something kind about Tom. He's told Tom that they don't want to nag him and that they want to solve a problem.

S is for Say what the problem is

Andrew: [Unemotionally, in a matter-of-fact tone] Here's the problem, Tom. Since you got your new phone last month, we've noticed that you have been getting messages late at night. We've been hearing the beeps on your phone. The other thing that happened last week was that we went into your bedroom really late and you were up playing a game on your laptop with some guys from California.

Tom: [Clearly getting irritated] So what, Dad! What's the big deal?

Andrew: Well, Tom, it was one in the morning, mate, and it was a school night.

Tom: School sucks!

Andrew: [Doesn't lose his place. He hasn't finished describing the problem — he still needs to describe to Tom what he's sees about his irritability at home] I can see how you might think we are making a big deal out of this, Tom, but I haven't quite finished telling you what else your mum and I have been seeing at home. So, if you'll give me a bit more time I would like to finish what I want to say. The third thing Mum and I have noticed is that you've been pretty crabby at home lately. In fact, your blow-ups at your sister have become more frequent. Not good, mate. We think it's probably because you're not getting enough sleep.

Tom: Oooawhh? Get real, you guys! What do you mean, 'not enough sleep'? I get heaps of sleep. This is crap. Who needs sleep anyway?

Andrew: [Endeavouring not to get derailed by Tom's frustrations] I know this must be upsetting for you that we want to bring this up. You might think that we are making a bigger deal out of this than is necessary.

Andrew has been interrupted a few times, but he hasn't lost his way. He knew he needed to get three things out: that Tom's been up late at night when he should have been sleeping he's been playing inappropriate games late at night, and he's been irritable at home.

Andrew's done a great job getting out what he wanted to say. He remained even-tempered and he could deal with Tom's interruptions. Now he needs to keep moving forward, and to tell Tom what he wants to change. Even though Tom has tried to minimize the problem and attempted to throw his parents off, he's hung in there so far. As we will see, getting any antsy teenager who is not used to this sort of sit-down conversation to remain 'in' the conversation is one of the more difficult parts of these types of discussions.

S is for Say what you want

Andrew: Mum and I have talked about this problem and we've decided that we want three things. One, we want everyone's devices to stay on their chargers in the kitchen overnight. Two, we want you to get one hour's downtime before you go to bed except on weekends and holidays. This means we want everybody off their screens including games, except for TV, by nine o'clock at night. Three, we want you to aim to get at least nine hours of sleep a night.

Tom: [Tom looks increasingly angry and resistant] This is crap! What do you mean I can't take my phone to my room? What is this, *prison*? Why can't I play my games? It doesn't have anything to do with you.

Andrew pauses to collect his thoughts. Remember, we can expect that Tom will not be happy about what his parents want to change. But Andrew stays calm and doesn't let himself be provoked by Tom's reaction. He remains focused on his part in the conversation. He is prepared and knows what to say to deal with Tom's reactions. He is about to utilize some of his taming the tiger skills by making further reflective statements in order to keep Tom in the conversation.

T is for Tame the tiger

Andrew: [Speaks with some grizzle in his voice — not angry but with some gravitas in what he is saying] Tom, I can see you're feeling angry about this. I can see how you might feel like we're fussing about nothing.

Tom:	[Still angry] But it's not fair! No other kid around here has parents like you guys. It's so unfair! It is! You want to take away my phone. You're trying to stop me using Facebook. All you want to do is control me. No one else's parents go on like this! You're such control freaks!
Andrew:	[Making a deeper reflective statement] So, you think we're being way too hard on you.
Tom:	[Looking noticeably righteous, and even angrier] *it's not fair!* Why do I have to get punished for having a phone?
Andrew:	[Clarifying what he is saying] We're not saying you can't use your phone or Facebook. What we are saying is that we need to know that we all use the internet properly and we think that you have been staying up late and not getting enough sleep, Tom. That's it.
Tom:	I do use the net properly. What are you talking about?
Andrew:	So you think we're trying to punish you for doing something that you're really interested in?
Tom:	Yeah you are!
Andrew:	I can see how it might look that way to you. I want to make sure you get enough sleep and you are not too tired for school or to exercise patience with people.
Tom:	[Snippy and snarling] Right ... *Sleep!* Oh, get over it! *I get enough sleep!*

Jane:	[Jane decides she's going to say something; she does not get distracted or angry, and she challenges Tom to take some responsibility] You feel annoyed because Dad and I want to set some limits. That's pretty normal. It's frustrating not being able to do what you want.
Tom:	[Upset, affronted and full of indignation] Yeah, but ... why can't I play my games when I want to?
Jane:	Well, I'm sure you can get involved in some other games in the same time zone, Tom, so that you are not online late at night when it's daytime for the other gamers. We're not saying you can't play games at all. Just not at night when you should be getting ready for bed or sleeping.
Tom:	This is crap.
Jane:	I can see you think we're making things difficult for you, Tom. [Remember, acknowledgement is not agreement]

Tom's parents have named how he's feeling and, by doing so, they've helped him 'get a grip' of his emotions. Sure, he still looks glum and pensive, but he hasn't flipped out or lost control. By making just a few reflective statements, Tom's parents have 'named' (not agreed) with what Tom is feeling and this has helped him to stay in the conversation with them.

Andrew and Jane have kept Tom on track with what they want to say. They continued to acknowledge what Tom may be feeling. While not agreeing with Tom, they stayed where they think Tom is at emotionally. At the same time, they stay firm about what they want. They are ready for Tom's objections. Instead of getting into an argument with Tom, their preparation has put them in a better position to handle Tom's flare-ups. They make their reasons for wanting to change Tom's behaviour clear: he is not looking after himself, he is not sleeping enough and his tiredness is resulting in him losing his temper with other people at home. Good job, parents! They are now ready to move on to the final past of the PASTA script.

A is for Agree

Andrew: Well, Tom, Mum and I are really proud of you for at least talking with us about this problem. We realize that you are not so happy with what we are asking you to do. We have been concerned about your irritability at home for a long time now and, in particular, your outbursts at your sister.

Tom: But this is so stupid.

Andrew: [Andrew lets this comment go through to the keeper] Okay so this is what is going to happen. We want you to organize things so you're in bed by ten on school nights and we want you to be off your iPad and phone by nine, unless there are exceptional circumstances. TV is fine after this time. At night, we will leave all our devices on the chargers in the kitchen. In the New Year, we will review this plan to see where things are up to. We think these arrangements will help everyone be a bit more tolerant towards with one another. [Wrapping up the conversation] Tom, Mum and I are really

	pleased that you can talk this through with us. We realize this is a big ask, but we need to see you not losing sleep to technology. If things change in time, we may change what we have talked about today, but we will have another chat about that before making those changes.
Tom:	[Thinking to himself 'As if!' but also half-acknowledging what his parents have said] Okay! Can I go now?
Jane:	Yeah, sure. [Tom gets up to leave] Thanks, Tom, you've done well.

Overall, Andrew and Jane stayed calm and firm. There was no yelling and no blaming; just clear direction about what was going to happen at their house and *how* it would happen. Tom is not in charge and his parents need to take control when their son's behaviour is not in his best interests. Even though Tom arced up at various times, they kept calm and collected, reflecting on the PASTA process and wending their way back and forth between Tom's objections and the PASTA script. There was no need to panic. They knew they would get there. Just like a sailing boat has to tack between positions to get from point A to point B, Andrew and Jane navigated towards a solution to resolve Tom's unacceptable behaviour. Although Andrew and Jane found it hard, they were able to control their own feelings and keep their bigger goal in mind: to resolve Tom's unacceptable behaviour.

By holding a tough conversation with Tom, they were able to negotiate the following:

» They agreed that Tom would be in bed by 10 p.m. during the school week to ensure he gets at least 8 to 9 hours' sleep a night.

» He would leave his phone recharging in the kitchen overnight.

> » Tom would get an hour's downtime — with no technology — before he went to bed.

As a result of this conversation Tom was both more alert and more patient with everyone at home. Some months after Jane and Andrew had taken these steps, Tom's school reports showed his marks had improved.

Case study 2: Emma, the late-night party-goer

Emma, the Coopers' fifteen-year-old daughter, has been coming home late from parties and not keeping in contact with her parents.

When challenged about her behaviour, Emma is likely to *feel* the following:

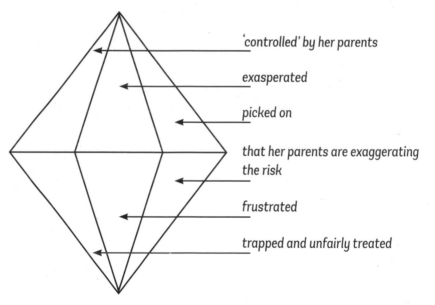

'controlled' by her parents

exasperated

picked on

that her parents are exaggerating the risk

frustrated

trapped and unfairly treated

These are all fairly *normal* reactions of a girl Emma's age, who is being confronted about her behaviour. She is going to find it tough to contain all her emotions when someone challenges her and her assumption that she can do what she wants. As Jane and Andrew work their way through PASTA, Emma's script is likely to be different to theirs. Emma might react in a number of different ways. She might:

» feel over-controlled

» be exasperated that her mother wants a say in what happens

» push back against her mother for being controlling

» tell her mother she is 'exaggerating'

» feel frustrated that she is being asked to change her behaviour

» feel trapped and unfairly done by.

Take 1: The train wreck

Here is the first attempt at a conversation with Emma.

Emma: [Emma approaches her mother, who is standing in the kitchen] Mum, what are you doing? I was meant to be at Ellie's five minutes ago.

Jane: [Turning around, caught on the hop] Sorry?

Emma: You said you would drive me to Ellie's. All the girls are staying there tonight.

Jane Look, I don't know what you're talking about at the moment. I don't even know where you're going. I need to talk to you about this party you want to go to next week.

Emma: What?! You said yes, there's nothing to talk about.

Jane: There are some things to talk about. And by the way, have you done the washing? Have you hung out any of the things you were supposed to earlier?

Emma:	[Emma begins speaking over her mum] That's beside the point! What's there to talk about, Mum? You said yes last night!
Jane:	Nothing's beside the point. And don't speak to me like that!
Emma	[Mocking her mother] No, *you* don't speak to me like that.
Jane:	I am not giving you a lift anywhere now! There is no chance I am going to drive you.
Emma:	Fine, I'm going to hitchhike! Fine, then.
Jane:	Fine!
Emma:	[Beginning to walk away] If I get abducted it's your fault.

Clearly, this conversation could have gone better. Emma caught her mother off guard and Jane just reacted. In the back of Jane's mind, she had wanted to have a conversation with Emma about the party she had previously asked permission to go to. She had hoped to have this conversation another time, but Emma's talking about going out prompted her to bring up the party. The conversation failed because Jane didn't hold back to manage things on her terms.

Take 2: A better run through

Jane is having a coffee with her girlfriend, Lisa. She's worried about losing control of Emma. Jane is feeling out of her depth trying to rein in Emma's increasingly escalating bad behaviour. Emma and Jane have had a pretty good relationship up until recently. But in recent months Emma has become increasingly menacing and horrible when she speaks to her mother. Emma has been talking with her mother about going to party that Jane is almost sure will involve drinking, older boys and no supervision.

P is for Prepare

Jane: She's just been such a handful lately. I can't seem to say anything without it turning into chaos. She wants to go to this party, but if it's like the last couple of times, it'll end up with her drinking, no supervision and that gang of Year 10 boys from the high school will probably be there.

Lisa: She's only fifteen, Jane, it's not time to fully let up yet. You'll have to see if you can try to get things back on an even keel. What about trying the PASTA stuff we learnt at the course?

Jane: But what if she gets antsy! I don't know how to handle it. I usually just get mad with her and it all goes pear-shaped.

Lisa: Look, we'll practice it if you like. I'll meet with you on the weekend and you can be yourself and I'll try to be her, and we can go from there.

Jane: Okay, I guess, we can give it a go.

Lisa: Okay, great.

A is for Appointment

Jane catches up with Emma as she is about to head off to school.

Jane: Emma, honey, before you go to school I want to make a time to talk with you about the party you've asked to go to. I was thinking that we could catch up later this afternoon before you go to swimming.

Emma:	Oh, come on, Mum, what do you wanna talk about? I can just go to it anyway, right!?
Jane:	[Jane, not wanting to get into the full conversation now] Well, look, I want to talk with you about this, and some other stuff as well. So how about we link up at about five o'clock at home. I can tell you what I'm thinking, and you can tell me what you want to say. I just need your agreement to be here, okay?
Emma:	I'll be here.
Jane:	Bye then.
Emma:	Bye!

Jane did well here. She could have been tempted to engage in the full conversation but she managed to tell Emma that all she wanted was an agreement to meet later on.

S is for Say something affirming (1)

Emma and her mother are sitting on the lounge at home.

Jane:	The first thing I want to say to you is how glad I am that we're able to sit and talk about this. It tells me that you're getting more mature and that you're able to negotiate about things.
Emma:	Why do we actually have to talk about the party? Why can't I just go?
Jane:	[Jane initially ignores Emma's detouring] Well, I know you've done well at school debating lately. So let's see if you can put these skills into action here. Do you think you will be able to hear me out?

Emma:	[Emma glares cynically at her mother] But why, Mum; I just want to go to Mel's party.
Jane:	I can see that you're keen to go to the party. I would like to work something out with you about doing that. If you can hear me out, then we can probably come to an agreement about you going to the party.
Emma:	[Emma sighs, folds arms, reluctantly agrees to engage]

Nice work from Mum. Jane ignores some initial detouring and stays on track to try to find something to compliment her daughter about.

S is for Say what the problem is (2)

Jane:	I want to describe what I believe happened when you went to Amanda's sleepover. I rang Melissa (Amanda's mother) about something else and found out that you'd left there to go to another party. I later learnt that you girls all went to Jodie's place while her parents weren't home and you were drinking in the flat downstairs. In other words, arrangements changed without me knowing.
Emma:	Why do we have to talk about this now? That was ages ago.
Jane:	Well, before you can go to this party I need to have a conversation with you about the arrangements. One other thing I want to discuss is that you haven't been answering my calls or texts when I try to contact you. There have been lots of occasions when I

haven't known where you are or who you were with.

Emma: [Emma looks surly, cynical, disinterested, and clearly tries to provoke a response] Can I go?

Jane: Okay, look honey, I know this is hard for you talking with me like this, particularly given we're trying a new thing here. You're fifteen, and I know that it is really normal for you to want to go out to parties and to hang out with your friends.

Emma: Yes! [Exasperated] Lately, I haven't been able to do anything! All my friends have been out having fun and I've been stuck at home. You're treating me like a ten-year-old.

Jane: You think I should be letting you make your own decisions?

Emma: Yes!

Jane: I need you to hear me out — just for a few minutes — without interrupting me. It's probably going to be hard for you to do this, but I really want you to try. Then you can have your say. Do you reckon you can hear me out for a few minutes?

Emma: Yes [aggressively/frustrated] I'll try. It's just that you are making me out to be the bad guy. Like I do bad things on purpose.

Jane: [Jane ignores Emma's attempted diversion] The other thing is that on the last two

	times we agreed that you would be home at a certain time and you actually got home quite late — once an hour and half late.
Emma:	Yeah, but Mum, nothing bad happened. I was fine. Everything was under control. We were just having fun.
Jane:	Yep, I hear that's how you see it.
Emma:	See, this is what I mean. This is why I don't tell you about everything because you just worry that everything's going to end up in some big accident. [Emma's body language indicates she is feeling a little histrionic — arms gesticulating, moving about, eyes rolling] Everything is such a big deal to you!
Jane:	I've got one more thing to say and then you can have your say. It's about us communicating when you go out. There's been a number of times when I haven't been able to contact you because your phone has been off. The last two times I've texted you, you haven't replied.
Emma:	[Emma throws head back, flicks her hair — looks exasperated] Yeah, but it's not my fault if my battery dies. It's not my fault. [Looks surly]
Jane:	You've got a charger, Emma — and I simply don't buy that it was flat.

[A bit of silence]

| Jane: | [Jane tries to summarize] So, they are the things that have been troubling me: you're |

sometimes not where you say you are, that you've been getting home way past the time we agreed and that you're out of contact.

Jane does well to stay focused on the facts. She clearly has a handle on what the problem is, and is able to state these by saying: 'arrangements changed without me knowing', 'We agreed that you would be home at a certain time and you were quite late' and 'The last two times I've texted you, you haven't replied.' She is now ready to move on to part 3 of Say.

S is for Say what you want (3)

Jane: I want to tell you what I want: I want to know where the party will be. I need to know the mother's number and I want to agree with you about a pick-up time. And I want you to respond to me when I text you. I will try not to disturb you while you are out with your friends, but I do need you to reply to me if I text you.

Emma: [Emma looks visibly indignant. She falls back into a pattern of escalating her emotional reactions, which usually culminates in her leaving an argument … but not this time]

Jane is clear about what she wants. Even though Emma is getting upset with her, she holds her line. She keeps firm and doesn't get sidetracked into any unnecessary tussles. Jane is following the PASTA process well. She knows that she may have to use some tame the tiger skills next to overcome any negative reactions Emma will have.

Emma:	But Mum, everything *is* a big deal to you. *Everything!* [Emma is looking visibly angry]
Jane:	Emma I know this is really hard for you. It must look like I am being overly strict.
Emma:	*Everything* is a big deal. You want to make the simplest things into such a drama.
Jane:	Yep, I can see how it might appear like that to you. [Jane waits]
Emma:	Why can't you listen to *me*? All I want to do is live my life, without you guys interfering!
Jane:	I can see you're getting frustrated. You think we are not letting you be independent and yet that's what you really want.
Emma:	I just want you and Dad to stop smothering me!
Jane:	You think we're doing too much and being too involved in what you think is your business.
Emma:	I'm fifteen and you need to start trusting me! You just can't treat me like I'm ten years old. All my friends are allowed to do this stuff, and their parents don't harass them like you harass me. [pleadingly, plaintively and starts to yell ...] All this stuff I'm not allowed to do just because you [makes inverted comma signs] 'care about me'. Aaaggh! [desperately] I can look after myself!
Jane:	[Jane is listening, but sees that Emma's getting more hysterical and gesticulating]

	Okay, I'm hearing that you're older, saying that I should be trusting you more; I agree.
Emma:	[Emma looks away in disgust or maybe even contempt. She looks pensive and worried and her eyes are moving from left to right while she wrestles with her feelings]
Jane:	[Waits and observes Emma stewing in her anger]
Emma:	But Mum … [weakly fading out]
Jane:	I think your dad and I are pretty much okay with the idea of you going to this party on the weekend, but I need those few things I have asked for and they are [counts on fingers]:

1. The mother's phone number.

2. Where the party will be.

3. A pick-up time.

4. I need your phone switched on and you need to message me back if I text you.

Emma:	[Aggressively] You're always in my face; you're always trying to control my life.
Jane:	I'm hearing that you are frustrated, Emma. You think what I am asking for is unreasonable. But if you can't contain that attitude we're going to have to stop this. I expect you to agree to those things I have asked for by the end of today if you want permission to go to this party. I need to have these things in place before I agree about you going to the party.
Emma:	[Visibly pulls back and retreats. She is

not happy, but she knows that they have
reached the end of the conversation]

Jane: [waits it out while Emma toggles]

Jane does really well here. She is not thrown by Emma's antics
and instead of the conversation escalating like it used to, and
ending with Emma walking off, Jane was able to use Tame the
tiger lines to hold Emma *in* the conversation. This is not only
better for Emma (helping her practise tolerating distress) but
also for Jane, who is able to get Emma to pull herself together.
Later that day Jane and Emma meet again.

A is for Agree

Jane: So, to sum up, let's go over what I think
             we've agreed about. I will come and get you
             at 11.30 p.m.

Emma: Yeah! [Cynically] You're not going to come in
             the house? That's so embarrassing.

Jane: Well, I'll text you when I'm five minutes
             away and you can meet me outside. Can
             you live with that?

Emma: Okay.

Jane: And your phone needs to be charged and
             switched on, Emma. I feel pretty happy
             about where we got to. You've done much
             better today. You can go to the party, and
             I hope you have lots of fun. You'll get me
             the contact for Ruby's mum. I'll text you
             at 11.25 p.m. and you'll come out the front
             to meet me. I'm really proud of you and
             the way you've mostly held it together
             today. It's been a big improvement on this

morning. Well done!

[Emma rolls her eyes and leaves]

Well done, Jane! She dealt with the issues at hand and maintained a level of equilibrium in the conversation. She came away with what she wanted, which was to make sure she had some contact with a supervising parent and to ensure that the lines of communication were open as far as Emma is concerned. Emma would have her phone working and she agreed to respond to her mother if she makes contact with her.

By holding a tough conversation with Emma, Jane was able to negotiate the following:

» Emma would give Jane the names of her friend's mother and their phone numbers.

» Emma agreed to a time when she would be picked up to come home.

» Emma agreed to keep her phone charged and switched on.

Case study 3: Seb, the lead-footed L-plate driver

Meet Seb, the Coopers' seventeen-year-old son, who is on his L-plates.

What Seb is likely to feel if his behaviour is challenged:
These are all fairly *normal* reactions of a young man Seb's age who is being confronted about his behaviour. He is not a kid with delinquent problems, but he's going find it tough to contain all his emotions when someone challenges him. As his parents work their way through the PASTA script he is likely to react in the following predictable ways:

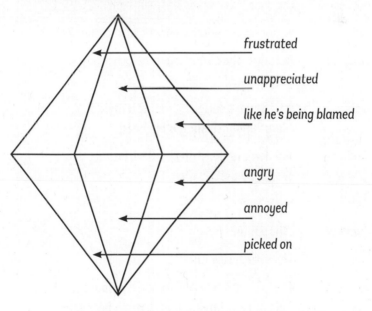

frustrated

unappreciated

like he's being blamed

angry

annoyed

picked on

» be frustrated that his parents want to further talk about what happened

» feel upset with his parents for questioning his ability

» say it was the other woman's fault

» accuse his parents of worrying too much

» attack and express his frustration that his parents want to control him in this way

» feel angry that his driving ability is being questioned and not willing to accept any blame.

Take 1: The train wreck

Andrew is reading the paper in the lounge room as Seb comes down the hallway on his way out the door.

Andrew:	Hey Seb, I need to talk to you about the other day in the car.
Seb:	No, I'm going. I don't want to talk about it.
Andrew:	No, wait, wait! You're not going to go out the door.
Seb:	Why not? So you can shout at me more?
Andrew:	Because what happened the other day was very serious!
Seb:	No it wasn't serious, Dad. You make everything into such a big deal!
Andrew:	You don't understand how serious it actually was!
Seb:	She's fine!
Andrew:	Who's fine?
Seb:	The little girl is fine!
Andrew:	The little girl is not fine; she's probably freaking out having bad dreams because you drove so close to her.
Seb:	It doesn't matter.
Andrew:	You are going to have to drive properly —
Seb:	[Seb interrupts] No, you're going to have to learn to drive properly!

Andrew:	... otherwise you're never going to get a licence.
Seb:	Well, why don't you try to teach me?
Andrew:	I'm not going to give you a licence —
Seb:	[Seb interrupts again] It's your fault!
Andrew:	... and no one else is going to give you your licence. I'm not even going to pay for your driving lessons if you aren't going to listen to me!
Andrew:	[Seth turns to leave] Do not go out that door! Do not go out that door! [Andrew sighs as Seb storms out the door]

Okay, that didn't go very well. Seb was clearly on his way out and Andrew caught him at an inconvenient moment. Given how the scene in the car the other day had caused such a big drama, it was always going to be unlikely that Seb would want to talk about what happened.

Take 2: A better run through

P is for Prepare

It's a few days after the driving incident in which Seb nearly hit a four-year-old girl, and where everyone in the car ended up screaming at each other.

Jane and Andrew are in the kitchen and are midway through a conversation about what happened, and what they're going to do.

| Jane: | The other day was nearly a disaster. Seb just reckons it's over with. We can't just let that one go. I keep having flashes of that little girl getting so close to being hit. |

Andrew:	I think you're right. This is one of those times we'll have to get onto this. It's not like it's the first time — he's been pretty well ignoring us for a month or so now. The other day could have ended up really badly. I want to make a time to have a chat with him whenever you're free. If we don't do it soon, the time will have passed and he will just assume it's all done and dusted. I don't want that to happen.
Jane:	Well, he's best in the morning, so it might be good to meet with him on Saturday about 10 a.m. or so?
Andrew:	Well, who's going to tell him?
Jane:	I will I suppose. I'll speak to him before I go to work in the morning.
Andrew:	Okay … I guess I can work on what we might say. Are you happy enough for me to have a go at the script stuff? I'll show you what we might go with by Friday.

Jane and Andrew know that they cannot just let this issue go. The other day was a serious accident waiting to happen and they know that unless it is dealt with, it may happen again and possibly result in a terrible outcome. They have resolved to hold a tough conversation with Seb to help him take some responsibility for what happened and to get some undertakings from him about his driving behaviour in the future.

A is for Appointment

Jane is just about to go to work and is on her way out the door when she turns to Seb who is finishing breakfast.

Jane: So, Seb, what have you got on at school today?

Seb: Not much.

Jane: The bus will be here soon.

Seb: Yep.

Jane: Before you go, I was wondering if I could make a time for Dad and I to talk with you about what happened in the car the other day.

Seb: What! We've already talked about it!

Jane: Yeah, I know we had a bit of a talk on the day it happened. But your dad and I want to get some things sorted out.

Seb: [Rolling his eyes] What's there to sort out? It's all good. That stupid woman shouldn't have been on the road!

jane: Well, could we meet at, say, 10 a.m. on Saturday?

Seb: Not ten. I'm going for an early surf with Billy.

Jane: What about twelve, then? You should be home by then.

Seb: [Grumbling, reluctant] I don't get it. Why do we have to do this?

Jane: Because Dad and I want to have a chat about it with you.

Seb:	What kind of chat?
Jane:	Now is not the best time to talk. Why don't you have a think about what you want to say in the meantime? We'll have a talk over some coffee on Saturday.

That's much better. Jane stays focused and does not get either detoured or distracted by Seb's protestations.

S is for Say something affirming (1)

It's Saturday at noon. Andrew and Jane are seated in the kitchen. Seb walks in.

Jane:	You right, Seb?
Seb:	[Seb comes to the table reluctantly] Oh all right.
Andrew:	Thanks for coming, Seb.
Seb:	Do we have to do this? We've already talked about it.
Jane:	We know this is not easy for you but I want to say it's really mature of you to come and talk about this. So, congratulations, and good on you for being here.
Seb:	[Sighing, groaning] How long is this going to take? I hate having these types of talks.
Andrew:	It won't take that long. So, first we just want to tell you what we saw happen the other day. We'll have our say and then you can have a say. It's going to take us a few minutes to say what we want to say. So it'd be good if you just heard us out and then

you can say some stuff. Reckon you could do that?

Seb: [Slouching in chair] Okay. Let's get on with it.

Andrew: The first thing I want to say is that your mum and I are on the same page with you about getting your licence. I also wanted to say that I wish it hadn't ended up in a yelling match the other day. If I could have my time over again, I wouldn't have got angry with you.

Seb: Yeah, you freaked me out yelling like that. And Mum was yelling in the back. I didn't know what was going on.

Andrew: I know, Seb. It was pretty hectic for all of us. One of the things I think we have in common is helping you to get your licence. We're on the same page with you about that one …

Seb: Yeah that's right. I want to get my licence so I don't have to have you guys always telling me what to do. Can't wait for that to happen. [turns his head around so he looking away]

Andrew: Well, it's true we do want to help you become the best driver that you can.

Andrew follows the script that he and Jane agreed upon earlier. The first few comments he needed to make included something good about Seb, to speak of his regret about how the other day turned out and to also make a same-page comment. He made all of these.

S is for Say what the problem is (2)

Andrew: [matter-of-factly] I want to start by telling you what we saw happen the other day. It's like bit of a replay of what happened. We need you to try to hear us out … we'll tell you when we're done and then you can have your say.

We were driving into town and coming into the 50-kilometre zone. I saw two cars coming down the hill on the other side of the road; they looked to be speeding up as they saw the 80-kilometre zone ahead. Up on the left I saw a woman already out on the road and getting a little girl out a car. It looked like she was going to step onto the road.

Seb: [Arcing up to avoid taking any blame for what happened] Yeah! That stupid woman. What sort of a parent does that? She shouldn't be allowed to have kids.

Andrew: [Andrew bookmarks his script to match Seb's frustration] Yes, she was pretty silly.

Seb: She was an idiot. She wasn't even watching her kid. That silly cow, what's she doing, getting her kid out like that? She shouldn't have been there.

Andrew: [Going with Seb's view of things for the moment] Look, you're probably right. She was pretty stupid — getting her kid out like that.

Seb:	You're making this out to be my fault, but if she wasn't there you wouldn't be on my case about this. I don't get why we're having to talk about this. Nothing happened. Can't we just leave this? Can't you guys just get over it? Nothing happened!

Andrew does well to stay on track with his description, despite being interrupted on a number of occasions. He is ploughing through with what he saw while acknowledging Seb, but not getting thrown off track. What Andrew notices is that Seb is getting pretty wound up (and he hasn't even got to the part where he's told Seb what he wants). Instead of moving on to the next part in PASTA, he does some serious tiger taming.

Andrew:	I think you're right in saying that a big part of what happened was that that woman shouldn't have been on the road. You know, it's not like we're saying you're a bad driver: we aren't saying that. You've done really well to get where you are. And we really want to help you. You seem really cranky; it's like you think the woman is the main problem and if she didn't have her kid on the road, there wouldn't be a problem.
Seb:	Yeah!
Andrew:	[Satisfied that Seb has been somewhat heard, Andrew goes back to his bookmark to continue to tell Seb what he saw] Okay … I just want to finish off describing what I saw. You right for me to go on?
Seb:	Yeah okay … How long is this going to take?

Andrew:	Not long, but probably longer if you keep interrupting me.
Seb:	Okay can we get on with it?
Andrew:	[Decides not to be provoked] So, what happened next was that I said, 'Seb, brake,' in about that tone.
Seb:	[Seb leaps on Andrew's comments; he sees it very differently] No, you didn't. You went, *'Seb, brake!'*
Andrew:	[bookmarks for a moment] Look, it's true I eventually did raise my voice. I did end up yelling. But first, I said, 'Seb, brake.' Then, I said, 'Seb, brake!' Then, as we got really close, I did yell, *'Seb, brake!'*
Seb:	Yeah, you really yelled. Freaked me out!
Andrew:	I did. And as I said to you, I regret that it got to that point. Nobody likes someone else yelling at them. [Andrew empathizes with Seb's experience] So, your reaction to get angry with me was kind of normal really. But we're not in that situation now. It's a bit calmer and we want to work things out so that it doesn't happen again. Now, Mum and I want to go over what happened to help you become a better driver.
Seb:	I don't want your help. I can drive now. I've got 60 hours up. I'm a good driver.
Andrew:	[Andrew doesn't get distracted, but goes a little way with Seb's view, without giving in] Well, you're pretty right. You certainly are getting more confident and you're heaps

better than when you started. Remember when you started you were bunny-hopping all over the place and you had trouble staying in the middle of your lane? Well, you've come a long way since then. You've really improved.

I just want to finish describing what I saw. So, we were heading into the 50-kilometre zone. I asked you to brake, you kept going, and in order to miss the girl and her mum you pulled towards the middle of the road. The two other cars coming the other way had to swerve off and you missed that little girl by about 60 centimetres. Then we had that big argument.

Seb: Yeah, Dad, but I missed her. [Seb tries to minimize]

Andrew: You did. Thank God for that!

Seb: [Still resistant] Get over it, Dad, I missed her, nothing happened. It's over. Are we done yet? How long's this going to take?

It's clear that Seb is really trying to minimize his part in the description. He's also being rude to his father. At this point Andrew thinks he can bookmark and that it might be good to hear from Seb.

Andrew: Well, what do you reckon happened?

Seb: I took evasive action. That's what happened.

Andrew: Yep, you did, you swerved, and you missed her. That was partly skill on your part, but probably a big dose of good luck as well.

Seb: So, you're saying that I'm a crap driver?

Andrew: [Andrew tries to stabilize things] No, I'm not
           saying that. You've impressed us a lot with
           the way you're driving has improved lately.
           As I said, you're managing to hold your
           position on the road.

Seb: [burning up] Yeah, well I've done 60 hours.

Andrew: I know, you're getting better all the time.
           [Andrew goes back to his bookmark to
           address how Seb's behaviour has been
           developing in to a bit of a pattern] But
           here's the thing ... lately there've been some
           other times when you've been hammering
           80 kilometres quite a bit.

Seb: Gee, Dad, you want me to drive at 50!?

Andrew: [Andrew ignores the provocation] Well, I've
           noticed your mother has been often saying
           to you that you need to slow down.

Seb: [Seb attempts to displace responsibility
           onto an outside factor] She's always
           nagging me and freaking me out. Telling me
           to *slow down, do this, do that*. She goes on
           and on. She never shuts up!

Andrew: [Reflects the emotion he sees in Seb and
           also uses a reflective statement] Look Seb,
           I can see you're getting really frustrated
           with this. Nobody likes other people talking
           to them about this kind of stuff. It's really
           hard to be the receiving end of other
           people's views like this. Let me recap our
           intentions here [expresses their common

purpose]. We really, really want to help you with getting your licence. It means a lot to us to help you get it right. You know what we know about you? We know that you really care about people and you'd want people that you're driving around to feel safe with you when you're in charge of the car they're in. The other day though, was a *big* problem. You see, Mum and I didn't feel safe.

Seb: [Still resistant] But no one got hurt.

Andrew: I know, and thank God they didn't. [Andrew now alerts Seb to how the incident has affected their relationship] The fact remains that we were scared. No, I'd say more like freaked out by what happened.

Here Andrew uses reflective statements to manage his son's anger and frustrations. He wasn't tempted to yell at Seb for expressing his feelings and instead he listened and tuned in to what Seb was feeling, without firing back at him.

S is for Say what you want (3)

Andrew: Let me tell you what we want out of this conversation. The first thing is that we need some acknowledgement from you about how serious the other day was. But we also want to get your agreement that you'll do what we ask and you'll drive more defensively in the future and that looks like this —

Seb: [Interrupting] This is SHIT! [Seb looks
                angry, glum, and resistant. Andrew draws
                back, bookmarks where he's up to, and
                pauses. He thinks it's time to do a bit of
                taming the tiger]

T is for Tame the tiger

Andrew: Seb, I know you'd rather not be here talking
                about this. And, given what I see in you,
                your reluctance to take any of this on
                board, I'm kind of wondering where that'll
                leave us with driving lessons in the future.
                [Andrew is purposefully ambiguous]

Seb: What do you mean?

Andrew: As I say. I reckon you're frustrated by us
                wanting to talk with you about this. But if
                we can't get this sorted we might have to
                stop driving lessons for a while.

Seb: What! [Seb looks noticeably righteous and
                angrier]

Andrew: [Andrew makes a further attempt to
                intervene] Seb, right now you can calm
                yourself down, and we can continue or
                we can have a break and talk about this
                tomorrow. It's your call. Do you reckon you
                can get in control of yourself or do you need
                to take a break?

Seb: [Seb doesn't respond. He has his arms
                folded, but he nods glumly for his dad to go
                on]

Andrew:	Okay. Now, I was talking about defensive driving: staying under the 80 limit and keeping the feelings of your passengers (to be safe) uppermost in your mind
Andrew:	[Andrew makes a further affirming comment, and he returns to the acknowledgement issue] Mum and I want to tell you that overall, we're very pleased with the skills you're showing. The other day was scary for us though. Did you hear me when I said for you to brake?
Seb:	Yeah!
Andrew:	Well, how come you didn't slow down?
Seb:	I thought I could get around them!
Andrew:	[Dad wants to evoke some acknowledgement from Seb] Seb, imagine if you had hit that girl, you could have killed her.
Seb:	[Still resistant, but less so] Yeah, but I didn't!
Andrew:	Let me tell you a bit more of what I saw happen … [Andrew is now really wanting to make the invisible, visible] What I saw, which really scared me, was the 'shocked' look on that little girl's face when she saw that we were getting near her. Hey, you know, you may not know this, but Mum was crying after that. We were both worried sick that you could have killed that girl. You would have had to carry that memory for the rest of your life. So, this conversation — uncomfortable as it might feel right now —

is, believe me, a small price to pay compared to the possibility of killing someone.

[Andrew waits]

[Seb doesn't know what to say and looks down]

Andrew: Let's take it as a bit of a given that the biggest part of what happened was the woman's fault. She had her kid on the road. The least part of the fault was mine and I shouldn't have yelled at you. I'm wondering if you took a part of responsibility for what happened — like in a pizza — what part could you take for your part? What could you have done differently? What part belongs to you?

[Andrew waits]
[Seb looks pensive, mentally toggling, waiting, reflecting]

Seb: I don't know. It was really hard. I didn't know what to do.

Andrew: Hmmm. Yep, it must have been pretty confusing.

Seb: I mean all of a sudden she was there. I had to miss her so I just tried to get round her. I didn't see the other cars swerving over till the last second.

[Andrew stays quiet]

Seb: It was hectic.

Andrew: [Andrew waits for split second to let Seb sit with this feeling] So, what could you have done differently?

Seb:	I don't know … listen to you, I guess. [Seb says this with more meaning this time]
Andrew:	[Waits and lets the silence become obvious] Okay, that's fine.
	Let's move on to the stuff you might do in the future. We also want you to drive a little bit slower — especially going into corners and for you to respond to what we tell you. So, if either Mum or I say, 'Slow down' or 'Brake', we want you to do it straight away.
Seb:	[Seb, thinking, and not quite agreeing just yet] Well, you two have got to do some stuff too! It's really hard for me to concentrate if you're both telling me what to do. And, Mum's the worst. Mum's telling me what to do, slow down, do this, watch out … I can't think!
Jane:	I didn't realize I was talking that much.
Andrew:	I can see that could be pretty distracting. So, you would like it if we didn't give so many instructions?
Seb:	*Yes!* Stop talking while I'm driving. I know what I'm doing. I don't need you and Mum telling me every little thing.
Andrew:	Okay, I think we can do that. I think Mum and I can limit what we're saying while you're driving. But we still need to know that you are going to drive at a safe speed to keep everyone safe, so it's not realistic for us to shut up all the time. We will try to talk less, but you need to remember that we're still the licensed drivers and we need to give your directions. Do you accept that?

Seb:	Oh ... all right.
Andrew:	I need to know that if we ask you to slow down that you'll do it immediately.
Seb:	Okay. [Partly reluctantly, but taking it on board]
Andrew:	Good; that'll do me. [Andrew is satisfied that Seb's heard him and agrees on some things]

Andrew did well in the last section in taming the tiger but in this section he did equally well to get to the point where he could outline what he wanted from Seb. He found a way to focus Seb's attention on where and how he could take some responsibility for what he had done.

A is for Agree

Andrew now turns to Seb to conclude and summarize what has been agreed upon.

| Andrew: | You've shown a great deal of guts to talk this through. We're very proud of you. I want to wrap up what we're agreeing about. We've agreed that Mum and I will try to talk less than we have been. We'll only talk if we think things are dangerous, or we want to say something encouraging, like if you've had a good drive and stuff like that. |
| | For your part, you can see from the other day that even though it was 'mostly' that woman's fault, you could have handled it differently by listening to me or by slowing down. You saying this gives me some inkling that you can take some responsibility for what happened. |

Finally, I think we've agreed that you'll try to not hammer 80 kilometres per hour, and you'll keep in mind that you need to make your passengers feel safe. We'll remind you about these two things for the next little while.

Some wins for you are that we'll try to take you out for more drives. At the end of our driving lessons Mum and I will try to tell you one or two things you've done well. Well, Seb, I really want to congratulate you on negotiating this with us.

Seb: Okay, okay … can I go now?

Andrew: Yeah sure.

Jane: Good on you, mate.

All in all, Andrew nailed this tough conversation. He handled the frustration in the room (including his own) and he was able to get some clear undertakings from Seb about his future driving behaviour.

By holding a tough conversation with Seb, Jane and Andrew were able to negotiate the following:

» Seb's acknowledgement of how unsafe his driving behaviour had been and how serious the incident with the little girl was.

» He agreed that he would drive more carefully and more defensively in the future.

» He agreed to listen to instructions from the licensed driver.

9

ADVANCED LESSONS IN TAMING TIGERS

In Chapter 6 we learned the two main ways you can tame tigers: by using *reflecting* and *contrast* statements. The purpose of these statements is to manage what's coming *at* you. These are your prepared lines you can use to defuse strong emotions. Through the inclusion of a savvy set of reflective statements, and by listening and reflecting, you should be able to reset most conversations to move on through the parts of PASTA. In cases where you can't, you need not lose heart. You can still reset the conversation by coming at things in another way.

Five advanced techniques for taming tigers

1. Say to your teen you can't possibly go on unless they settle down.

2. Name the pattern they are re-enacting — such as regularly blaming someone else — and ask them not to go into it.

3. Be curious by digging a bit deeper emotionally and asking a question.

4. Ask for 'more' responsibility from them.

5. If they insult you, don't just sit there like a stunned mullet.

1. Say to your teen you can't go on unless they settle down

If you are in the process of a tough conversation and have used several reflective and contrasting statements yet your teen is still becoming increasingly upset, you might try hitting the reset button by asking for their permission to go on. In other words, you put the responsibility on them and say that if they can't or won't calm down, you just won't be able to continue. You might try saying something like:

> I have tried really hard to hear your frustration; I can see it's really hard for you to work this out with me. I get that. But I don't know what else to do. I guess if you can't get a grip, we'll have to stop this conversation.

> *Or:*

> I hear you are angry — maybe even a bit affronted that I have even dared to bring this up. I can't really go on here without your cooperation. So, what do you want to do?

If part of what you are doing is having a conversation about a future event (for example, their use of technology or their wish to go to a party) chances are that your signal to stop the conversation will pull them up in their tracks. By saying you can't possibly go on under these circumstances, you're signalling to them that they need to exert some self-control. Here are two more examples:

> I'd really like to continue by treating you like a nearly grown-up person, and I want to believe that we can work this out, but I can't do that unless you give me permission to keep going. You know, part of you becoming a young adult is that I can believe you won't lose it and that you have some capacity to hold it together. So, what would you like to do?

Or:

> I can't go on and I guess we'll have to stop unless you can calm down. I'd like to hear from you in a moment, but if I can't finish what I'd like to say, then I don't know what to do ... I guess if you can't stop yourself from getting mad, then we'll just have to finish things up for the day.

If your teen says something like, 'But the party's on Saturday!' you can respond by saying, 'Well, it's up to you.' Hopefully, they'll pull their head in enough for you to continue.

2. Name the pattern they are re-enacting

Another way to help your teen assume some better control of themselves is to name a pattern of behaviour they usually adopt in order to get their own way or to avoid facing their responsibilities. Just by stating what you see happening, you can reset the whole conversation. See the example below:

You know I get it that you feel like we're picking on you. But what I also see a lot is that when we have these kinds of conversations the same things keep happening over and over. I bring up something that you don't want to hear, you get upset — even really angry — and say it has nothing to do with me and then you walk out. This is a pattern I have seen many times when we speak like this. I'd ask you not to go into this pattern. I want you to give this conversation one more try, otherwise if you can't pull yourself together, we'll have to stop, and we won't be able to negotiate what you want any more.

3. Be curious by digging a bit deeper emotionally

It is sometimes very difficult for teenagers to tune in to their own emotions. We have to remember that this is a growth area for them. While they may express frustration, what might underlie that emotion is actually fear or anxiety. For example, Seb, our lead-footed L-plater, may have been frightened by almost hitting a pedestrian but pride stopped him from saying that. When Andrew picked him up on his behaviour, he came across as prickly but really he could have been quite scared by what happened.

At these times it can be best not to pursue the anger expressed but to tune in to the emotion you suspect your teen feels but might not be so crash-hot at expressing. Rather than just reflecting their feeling as you see them *expressing* it, you might venture to go deeper. For example, if your teen is being really prickly, it might *look* like they are angry but you could choose to explore their emotion more deeply by saying:

> You know, I'm curious ... nearly colliding with someone like that is a bit of a freaky thing to happen. If that happened to me, I reckon I would feel a little scared or freaked out by what happened. I imagine most people would feel that way. I'm just wondering if it's not just anger that you're feeling but also maybe a small dose of being scared as well.

This strategy involves you coming across as interested or curious about what *could be* happening and, by doing so, you are asking them to consider things differently.

Here's another example:

> I know it's hard for you to stay in here in this conversation and speak about this stuff. It's not easy but I can't help but feel that if we were to successfully work something out you might feel pretty good about that. You will have stayed in this process and achieved something.

As a parent, if you can try to tune in to what emotions anyone might have in your teen's situation not only do you normalize what your teenager might be feeling, you also connect with what they are experiencing. This can help to re-establish the tone of a tough conversation.

4. Ask for more responsibility from them

It goes without saying that some young people will 'try it on' by getting overly uppity or disproportionately angry, to get you off their back or to confuse you in your attempts to solve a problem.

You'll remember that one of the things we discussed earlier was that self-control is on a continuum. In other words, it's not like some people have it and some don't. We also learned that, as young people get older, their ability to pull themselves together improves with age. So, you're within your rights to ask them to show this increased ability (compared to when they were a child) to exert better self-control.

Many young people feel like home is a place where they can unleash their feelings without restraint, simply because they can and that's what they're used to doing. But I want to remind you that you are not there to be anyone's doormat and you should expect them to pull themselves together.

It's one thing to hear them out by acknowledging their feelings and by helping them wrestle with their strong emotions. But if they are not responding to your efforts to hear what's going on for them, you may have to challenge them. By this, I mean you're asking them to dig deep into their personal reserves — to exert the self-control that you know they possess — and to respond to your belief that they *are* up to the challenge. Some examples are listed below:

> You know, I reckon you can do this. You're not ten years old any more, in fact you're sixteen, so I'm expecting more from you. I can hear you're angry — maybe even a bit embarrassed — that I have even dared to bring this up. I can see that. But you're growing up and I suppose I'm expecting that you can handle this kind of thing. If you don't mind, I'd like to continue.
>
> *Or:*

I hadn't quite finished describing what I saw happen the other day. Do you think you could let me go on for a minute or two? I know you have the ability to keep yourself from spinning out. I want you to exercise some self-control while I finish what I am saying.

Or:

You can hang in here, you know. I believe in you and we can sort this out. I need more from you than the regular act of you just flipping out when you don't like what I'm saying.

Or:

I want to challenge you to stay in here with me. I will let you have your say in a moment. Right now though I need to finish describing what I want out of this conversation. So, if you could let me finish that would really help.

5. If they insult you, don't just sit there like a stunned mullet

If your teenager gets so frustrated that they insult or swear at you, you'll need to respond. It can be shocking when your teenager does this and it's often hard to know what to say at that moment. Sure, you might take umbrage and tell them off. But there are other ways to regain control of a situation. Keeping in mind that most teenagers spit insults when they are feeling pretty miserable in themselves or backed into corner, look them straight in the eye and say:

You must have had a pretty bad day to
feel the need to say something that nasty
to me when we are trying to work out a
solution to a problem. I hope you feel
better.

In her book on everyday manners, author Amy Alkon says that by
expressing sympathy for a spiteful insulter, you've accomplished
three things:

» You have refused to accept being turned into their
victim.

» You have come off classy and bigger than they are.

» You have sent the message that what you talking about
is not about you, it's about a real-life problem that you
want to sort out with them.

One of the main challenges for parents of teenagers is holding
them *in* a tough conversation. As we've seen, most teenagers
who behave badly do so out of habit and not because they are
not capable of containing their frustration. By assuming that
they can bring a degree of self-control to any encounter, you are
manoeuvring the conversation in such a way that your teen will
have no choice but to put their best foot forward. Sometimes we
need the people who love us to help us to do our best ... and we
need this more at the times when we look ugly.

In the next chapter I have included some instructions for
filling out PASTA scripts. There's a completed worksheet by the
Coopers with annotations to show my thoughts, and there's a
blank worksheet for you to use.

In essence

» When your teenage son or daughter gets on their high horse there are some things you can do to hold them accountable to maintain self-control.

» Sometimes that means that we need to challenge them to assume better self-control.

» The advanced strategies for taming tigers in this chapter require you to be strong. Knowing that you have some 'holds' (as in wresting) you can use to contain what's going on will help.

10

INSTRUCTIONS FOR USING SCRIPTS

We'll first take a look at how the Coopers completed one of their worksheets, so that you have something to compare to. This is the worksheet they completed before they talked to Tom about his use of the internet at night.

I've annotated what they have written so you can see my thoughts (in brackets). Following this completed worksheet, there is a blank set of worksheets for you to complete. (By the way, this is the one section of the book that my publisher and I agree you can copy so you can practise using the worksheets for as long as you need to.)

Preparing what you are going to say is a very important part of the process. Once you've had a few PASTA worksheet conversations to prepare yourself with, you probably won't need to prepare as much, but for the first few times it's essential so that you don't lose your place or get side-tracked. When you've filled the sheets in, I suggest practising the conversation with a friend. Doing this will better enable you to manage your teen's reactions.

Tough conversation preparation worksheet

P is for Prepare

What's the problem?

Use the CPR model to describe the problem: Content, Pattern, Relationship.

Content

What has actually happened? *(Get the basics stated on paper.)*

> He's staying up late, not getting enough sleep and cranky with others at home.

Pattern

How often does it keep happening? Every day? Twice last week? *(State how much and how regularly the problem has happened.)*

> Lately a lot, but the last two months have been the worst since he's got that last game!

Relationship

What does your teen's behaviour do to the relationship between them and others in their life? *(Say who is affected + what effect was felt.)*

> He's short tempered and argumentative. He lost his temper with his sister last week. She cried after he hit her.

What do you want?

(Say exactly what you want the outcome to be and that it's part of their job.)

> A less fraught home life. For him to sleep so he will learn better at school.

Negotiables

What aspects of the problem might you be willing to negotiate about?

> He can still play video games but at reasonable times of the day, not late at night. I'm happy to negotiate the time we meet to discuss this, but we are going to talk, no matter what.

Bottom lines

What are you not willing to negotiate about?

> Has to go to bed by 10 p.m. — and he has to be off the net by 8.30 p.m.

Stop gaps

Consequences for not negotiating an agreement.
(Establish a line in the sand.)

> Take his phone from him. Limit his internet access.

A is for Appointment

Remember, your purpose is to flag the issue with your teen. There are three essential elements to flag: What do you want to talk about? Where do you want to meet? At what time?

Mum and I want to talk with you about your internet usage and staying up late. We'd like to meet with you tomorrow (Saturday) at 10 am.

S is for Say something affirming

Your purpose is to help them feel good about themselves and for attending the meeting.

We've noticed you've had teachers saying you're good in classroom debates. The thing we most admire about you is the effort you've been putting into the social justice group at school. Thanks for meeting with Mum and me today.

S is for Say what the problem is

Your purpose is to paint a non-judgemental picture of what's going on.

We have noticed you've been staying up a lot in recent months. We've observed you being more short-tempered. We've seen how hard it is for you to get up in the mornings. We've noticed you're nodding off during the day and we think that's because you're sleep deprived. Lately, you've been crabby at home — especially with your sister.

S is for Say what you want to happen instead

Your purpose is to tell them, in clear language, what you want to see happen in the future. *(Write clear points.)*

- We want you off the net by 8.30 p.m.
- We don't want you playing violent video games on weeknights.
- We want you to do something else instead: read, talk with your friends on the phone.
- We want your phone on the charger in the kitchen overnight.

T is for Tame the tiger

You can tame the tiger by using at least three reflective statements and one contrast statement. Some examples of each are below.

Reflective statements

These help them get in touch with how they are feeling and shows that you understand them.

- So I sense you're [annoyed] with us for wanting this.
- I'm guessing you're [frustrated] that we want to put these limits in place.
- You're [cranky] that we're thinking like this.
- If I were you, I'd feel [what we're asking for] is unfair.
- I'm guessing that you think we're making a big deal out of nothing.
- I can see you're [mad] at my effort to bring this up.

Contrast statements

These clarify what it is you want by saying what you don't want.

- *We don't want to stop you playing your games. We do want you to do this on weekends only.*
- *We're not saying you can't play these games. We are saying they don't need to keep you up at night.*
- *I'm not accusing you of doing this on purpose. I am saying that what happened last week was a problem.*

A is for Agree

Your purpose is to describe what you have agreed. If you can name what's in it for them, as well as yourself, then good.

Okay, let's look at what I think we've agreed about:

1. *No games during the week.*

2. *No internet access after 8.30 p.m.*

3. *Phones go on the charger overnight.*

Here is your own worksheet for preparing a tough conversation.

Blank tough conversation preparation worksheets

P is for Prepare

What's the problem?

Use the CPR model to describe the problem: Content, Pattern, Relationship.

Content

What has actually happened?

_____

_____

_____

_____

_____

_____

_____

Pattern

How often does it keep happening? Every day? Twice last week?

_____

_____

_____

_____

Relationship

What does your teen's behaviour do to the relationship between them and others in their life?

_____

_____

_____

_____

_____

_____

_____

What do you want?

Negotiables

What aspects of the problem might you be willing to negotiate about (e.g. pick-up time)?

_____

_____

_____

_____

_____

_____

_____

Bottom lines

What are you *not* willing to negotiate about (e.g. rude behaviour)?

_____

_____

_____

_____

_____

_____

_____

Stop gaps

Consequences for not negotiating an agreement (e.g. not drive them places, limit internet access).

_____

_____

_____

_____

_____

_____

_____

A is for Appointment

Your purpose is to flag the issue with your adolescent. There are three essential elements to flag:

- » Tell them what you want to talk about.
- » Tell them where your meeting will be.
- » Arrange a time for your meeting.

S is for Say something affirming

Your purpose is to help them feel good about themselves and also about attending the meeting.

S is for Say what the problem is (using the CPR)

Your purpose is to paint a non-judgemental picture of what's going on.

S is for Say what you want to happen instead

Your purpose is to tell them, in clear language, what you want to see happen in the future.

T is for Tame the tiger

Reflective statements

_____

_____

_____

_____

_____

_____

Contrast statements

_____

_____

_____

_____

_____

_____

A is for Agree

_____

_____

_____

_____

_____

_____

In essence

» The PASTA method is a step-by-step approach used successfully by mediators in one form or another for resolving disputes.

» By preparing a script ahead of time you can approach the problem with your head screwed on.

» By having a script to refer to, you can move methodically towards your destination.

11

THEY WON'T KNOW HOW TO NEGOTIATE UNLESS SOMEONE SHOWS THEM

Someone in one of my courses said that what I was essentially teaching was anger-management for parents. I'd like to think our parenting courses offer more than that! I did see what this parent meant. One thing I do know is that without someone showing us what to do, we will tend to do what we've done before. Unless someone teaches us another way of negotiating a problem, we will not replace what we do now with a better way in the future.

At least part of growing up is being able to 'hold our nerve' under pressure, to take turns in a conversation (at a simple level) or to tolerate a level of distress, in order to work out how to respond if we think someone's being a complete nong. Sometimes we will need to juggle strong feelings to do so.

In fraught social encounters, we can often act out of habit.

But if we know we have an alternative route, we can go that way. In any event, if we know what else is possible we have options. Having a systematic method can make all the difference.

For teenagers, unless they get good practice at negotiating real-life circumstances, where real-life emotions are at play, they will struggle in containing their emotions and reactions. They won't learn the skills involved in negotiating.

We teach teenagers how to drive a car by taking them out for many hours of practice, so they can eventually drive by themselves in all conditions. But when it comes to teaching them to negotiate, it is unlikely that most teenagers get anywhere near this amount of training. Unfortunately, I don't think there are many places where young people can learn the skill of negotiating. Certainly, nothing on TV or in the media leads me to believe that they will learn how to handle themselves in tough encounters from there. Schools are doing more in this department these days, but they are probably not going to be able to provide the real-life circumstances.

More recently, we have been schooled to stick up for ourselves so much that, at times, it is difficult to relinquish our personal wants and needs for the good of the group. I have seen increasing instances where teenagers appear much more aware of their individual rights to the exclusion of others. However, living in a family often involves compromising and coming up with a workable solution.

Experts in mediation and workplace relations say that part of the problem about problems in the workplace is that people put off resolving them because they are worried that other people will get angry. When we are rushing about or feeling harassed ourselves we can just react and do the first thing that comes to mind. It's difficult *not* to react to our children's difficult behaviour and shoot from the hip.

PASTA offers a selection of strategies for laying out a problem. It is also a strategy for you to do things differently. If you get the chance to use the script sheets, and I hope you do, I expect you will find that just by completing them you will lessen any emotions at play in challenging your teenager's behaviour. By writing down your thoughts it will help you determine what really is at stake. Getting clear about what really *is* the issue can take the emotion out of it and help you to work out reasonable steps to resolve problems. Sometimes the very act of writing down your thoughts in the form we have looked at, helps you to get perspective — which, as it turns out, can be very different *after* writing your script compared to your initial thoughts.

Here is what other people have said about writing down their thoughts using the PASTA script:

» 'It clarifies the problem and minimizes side issues.'

» 'It allows us to anticipate and have a method for dealing with our teenager's reactions.'

» 'It provides a map for where we'll go in the conversation following PASTA.'

» 'It helps us decide the attitude we will take into the conversation.'

As you have seen, by far the hardest part of PASTA is how to manage a teenager who starts to get antsy or who doesn't see eye-to-eye with you about the problem *you* want resolved. While it is entirely normal that your first reaction would be to fire back, I hope you can see by now that this is just one way for you to respond.

Taming is exactly that — it's *you* doing some things to keep the temperature in a zone when everyone is still thinking. Now that you have PASTA, you have options that don't require you to let loose or be the ogre. By preparing well and by navigating appropriately, you can pull other conversational rabbits out of a hat. Worst coming to worst, you can use advanced taming techniques or simply call the conversation off until either one of you can bring a cooler head to proceedings.

Remember the pilots we spoke about earlier? They do their job matter-of-factly, and with a procedure in mind. That's how *you* have to be if you want the best out of a tough conversation with your son or daughter. Treat it matter-of-factly and without emotion. If you behave like this, not only will your teens learn to negotiate by trading views but you will teach them that the default need not be screaming or yelling at each other.

Of course, we can all get angry and make threats when situations get tough. Or we can sit down and talk about what is happening. It's worth remembering that you are going to get more bang for your buck if you hold purposeful conversations, aimed at working out a solution to unacceptable behaviour.

My view is that there are too few models for teenagers to negotiate and make peace — skills that will not only help them deal with life, but which might also make their lives less fraught — particularly when they form lifelong relationships down the line. Watching their parents approach problems like this time after time, teens will be better equipped to maintain sustained and mature relationships. They will learn that differences *can* be talked over and often resolved. Negotiating is about give and take. Sometimes you win and sometimes you don't — that's life.

As we have discussed, we can expect that the vast majority of young people will develop the ability to rein in their behaviour and this will improve with each passing year. They'll get better at tolerating distress and at putting things in proportion year on year. I truly believe that PASTA conversations are a great way of resolving many differences. It teaches them a process for nutting out solutions to problems they may experience with others in their future — and it does it in a way that does not necessarily involve heightened emotions.

If a big drama is about to happen, use your attachment!

For some problems, PASTA-type conversations may not always be the best tool to use. These problems are generally ones that have been in the making for many years, ones that Mum or Dad have let go because they didn't know what to do about them. I'm talking about the increasing use of aggression that eventually leads to an assault, or where a girlfriend becomes pregnant after escalating behaviour or where a teenager gets suspended or expelled from school after a period of lead-up incidents.

You may have seen your son or daughter heading down a particular path, and hope that nothing happens — and sometimes it doesn't. Many parents, even though they can see an accident in the making, feel paralysed from taking any action and they hold back from intervening — hoping that something will change to make things different. The sad thing is that a lot of the problems could have been avoided if action had been taken earlier.

I have seen the aftermath of this situation so many times, parents who present with family wreckage that could have been avoided had they confronted their teenager at an earlier juncture. I am not saying that the problem is always down to parental omission. Like many things in life, there are other variables at play that have little to do with 'the parent', such as exposure to social media, fads and fashions, unfortunate friendships and heaven forbid, free will!

What I am saying is that some teenage problems can be lessened if Mum or Dad took steps early on. My own view is that too many young people are not made aware of the effects of their behaviour on others or on their own reputation — and they need to be.

A lot of us tend to underplay the effects of behaviour on others and themselves in a situation. You'll recall back in Chapter 4 when we looked at describing a problem using CPR, which not only identifies the facts of the problem but also how it is affecting others. Well, it works in the reverse as well. You can leverage *your* relationship to affect change in them. You can use the attachment you have formed with your teen to your advantage to influence their behaviour.

To be entirely blunt, I would have thought there are some occasions when it would be far less painful to inflict some discomfort on them now, by talking about how their actions will affect others, than after a less desirable outcome has actually happened.

For example, talking with your teen about how their sexting or vandalism or bullying is affecting others before it gets bad is a much more effective — and less painful — option than waiting until it ends up in grief. And, though you may think that what I am saying amounts to emotional pressure on teenagers I would add this. At eighteen, when your teen is seen as an adult in the eyes of the courts and the community in general, these systems will no longer give your son or daughter the benefit of the doubt they might have done when they were younger.

Although eighteen is still a very young adult, I believe that parents should use their relationship to positively pressure a young person to behave better, when it's appropriate. So, pressure appropriately dished out is a fair enough thing to do in my books. For example, you might say something like:

> You know when you hurt your sister like you did [by belting her with your fist] my heart really sinks. I worry deeply about the person you're turning into and, whether, at some stage in the future, you'll end up doing that to your wife.
>
> *Or:*

I was really shocked to see that you would post those pictures of yourself on Facebook. You are a precious person to us, but that cheapens you in the eyes of some people; we know you're way better than that, but not everyone would think that way.

Or:

Did you know that the police can arrest you for defacing people's property by spraying graffiti the police can arrest you? I just don't know where you learnt that. You certainly didn't learn that from Dad or me. I expect that many people would wonder what kind of family you come from. What you are doing reflects badly on all of us. I want you to think about that the next time you want to do something like that.

As we have said, an important part of being a parent is outlining what's appropriate, and what's not. You will sometimes need to tell them these hard truths, because it is important to help them get perspective when they are behaving badly. Generally speaking, you know far more about the appropriateness of social behaviour than they do. Pulling up your teenager for their behaviour means helping them get practice at making ethical decisions and questioning their actions. It's also about pointing out the consequences of what they do, perhaps in regards to the law, or on their own reputation, and how this might affect their future work prospects.

Consequences

By now, you'll have worked out that my view is that young people can make increasingly mature and sophisticated choices and are also capable of managing their strong emotions. You can leverage this latent capability by demanding this of them. You can ask them to act like the nearly-adult people that they are, and to ask for 'more' from them.

But I'm not so naïve to believe that there won't be times when you will have to implement 'Plan B'. Either your teenager won't negotiate or they will blatantly breach agreements. If they do this you may have to pull rank on them. In my view, pulling rank may be absolutely necessary — especially if you believe that their safety is at stake.

Unpleasant consequences happen in the real world when people misbehave: people lose their licence, people get fired and, in some circumstances, some are sent to prison. Even though you can and should try to do everything to work inside a reasonable framework where things can be talked out, there might be times when your teenager will not be open to acting maturely and will be defiant.

In these cases, both logical and natural consequences may apply.

Logical consequences are where you take an action that is related to the situation, like not taking them on driving lessons if they don't drive more safely or withholding your permission for them to go to a party if they refuse to agree about a reasonable pick-up time.

Natural consequences are where things happen when you do nothing. For example, if they don't call you as they said they would to organize being picked up — and you do nothing. Then they have to wear the consequence of you not coming to pick them up. Or, if you don't remind them that they have to pay for a school excursion by a deadline and they miss the excursion. In these cases, by not doing anything you are teaching them to be more responsible by looking after things that are theirs to look after.

In extreme cases your teenager may behave so badly that it affects you or someone in your home so that you can't live together safely. Eventually, you may have to get outside help. Often an experienced professional can help build bridges, while supporting you through a difficult patch. Ultimately you may have to ask your teenager to leave your house.

CONCLUSION

Late in 2014, UNICEF published a large study of parenting called *Hidden in Plain Sight*. That report identified a large swathe of children and teenagers still regularly hit by their parents in over 190 countries. In fact, the research showed that 60 per cent of children aged between four and fifteen were physically struck on a regular basis as a form of discipline. The corresponding finding was even more staggering. *Seventy per cent of the parents who did the hitting did not want to use corporal punishment*; they just didn't know what to do instead.

If I can give you something that minimizes the need for you to use excessive force to manage your teenager's behaviour, I will feel like I've done my job.

Certainly, when I have taught the information that is in this book in communities, both family professionals and parents have often wondered what the research question for it would be. An obvious question in any parenting program is normally, 'Has the young person's behaviour improved?' But I think a more realistic question is, 'Do parents believe they are more effective in doing their job?' Even though a teen's behaviour might improve, it doesn't necessarily mean a parent feels effective. At the same time, a parent might feel more effective but their teen's behaviour doesn't necessarily improve. In other words, good behaviour is not necessarily an automatic outcome of good parenting. It is fair to say that some behaviour is hard to reverse in teenagers. I don't mean to put a downer on proceedings here as we finish up. But really, I don't know any program that is a magic bullet for some really wayward teenagers. Their talent for behaving badly may be too entrenched across many years and be plain resistant to change.

What I do think, though, is that it is possible for you to believe that you are doing a half-way decent job — even if you do not turn your teen's behaviour around. *Your confidence in what you are doing doesn't have to correspond with your teenager's improved behaviour.* It'd be good if it did, but it does not mean that you are doing a second-rate job if you don't see improvements. It might mean that their behaviour — having developed over a period of time — will take more time (months or years) to come good. Remember, that the older they get, the more formed their personalities become. That's the good news — and the bad news. But the really important news is that you can still feel a competent parent even if you have rough ride with your teenager; the two things don't have to perfectly align.

Another important point to make here is that teenagers need training and the opportunity to do things differently. In other words, *if young people don't get the training,* as they would at football or netball, they won't learn how to haggle with the competing thoughts *inside* of themselves. My own view is that when they don't receive the training and the practice at wrestling with their strong feelings, they won't cope as well in life's different situations as well.

Resolving problems with teenagers who, at the end of the day, have free will, is complicated. I have met many young people coming from otherwise terrific family environments, who make unexpected bad judgement calls. It's not *always* about parenting.

Sometimes it's the world, the culture and young people's freedom to make choices that are bigger factors than any one parent's influence on their teenager's behaviour.

Best of luck with those (planned) tough conversations ahead of you.

In essence

» Some problems with your teenagers will require you to sit down and confront their behaviour by having a conversation about it. These may be problems you've been ignoring for a while but that have now settled into patterns that you would like to change.

» To do PASTA well, initially it's important to prepare. Clarify the problem using CPR (content, pattern, relationship), think about how your teenager may react, write out what you're going to say (using preparation worksheets) and practise on a friend if you can.

» Some problems cannot be resolved using PASTA and for these you may need outside help.

» Teens need training and practice in wrestling with strong emotions in order to learn how to manage them.

» If you practise conflict resolution in a calm and matter-of-fact way, listening to others' views and being firm about your own, you will teach your teen negotiating skills that will last them a lifetime.

» Sometimes there are problems that don't relate to good or bad parenting. It is not always about the parenting.

ACKNOWLEDGMENTS

I dedicate this book to my mother and father for the warmth and love they gave me and my brothers (Paul, Chris and David). My parents provided us with a warm and loving family life. In our early years our family was a place for us boys to thrive and feel confident to take up life's challenges. I also wish to pay tribute to my aunties and uncles from whom I sought advice and guidance over the years.

To my lovely wife, Simone, and our much-loved children — Dom and Isabelle — I acknowledge your patience with me these past years in covering for me when 'life got hectic' as I was writing this book. Simone, thank you for the occasional reading of the manuscript and your comments — quite apart from your support of me personally in writing this book.

To my staff at Parentshop, Caitlin, Kelley, Helen, Melissa, Fiona, Amanda and Philip, thank you for your encouragement and hard work. All of you have kept me focused on putting something together to make a difference to the lives of families. To my colleagues Brad Williams, James Brown, Michael and Rebecca Lines-Kelly, Stephen Luby, Terry Laidler, Rob Steventon, Rob Whiting, Peter Chown and Tom Phelan, you have given me your time in mentioned and unmentioned ways.

I also acknowledge the contribution of the now thousands of family professionals we have trained in Engaging Adolescents and who work with parents day in and day out. You are in many ways the unsung heroes in family life and your stories have added to the colour in this book. You are the 'parents in lieu' of parents who lack a closer connection with their own families.

To my editors and all the staff at Exisle I say thank you.

FURTHER READING

BIBLIOGRAPHY

Alkon, A. (2014). *Good Manners for Nice People Who Sometimes Say F*ck*. St Martins Press, New York.

Caspersen, D. (2015). *Changing the Conversation: The 17 principles of conflict resolution*. Profile Books, London.

Clinton, W. (2004). *My Life*. New York: Knopf Publishing Group, New York.

Dillon, P. (2009). *Teenagers, Alcohol and Drugs: What your kids really want and need to know about alcohol and drugs*. Allen & Unwin, Sydney.

Doidge, N. (2010). *The Brain That Changes Itself: Stories of personal triumph from the frontiers of brain science*. Scribe, Melbourne.

Fedler, J. (2014). *Love in the Time of Contempt: Consolations for parents of teenagers*. Hardie Grant, Melbourne.

Giedd, J. N. (1999). 'Development of the human corpus callosum during childhood and adolescence: A longitudinal MRI study', *Progress in Neuro-Psychopharmacology & Biological Psychiatry* 23: 571-588.

Giedd, J. N. (2004). 'Structural magnetic resonance imaging of the adolescent brain', *Adolescent Brain Development: Vulnerabilities and opportunities*. 77–85.

Giedd, J. N., J. Blumenthal, et al. (1999). 'Brain development during childhood and adolescence: A longitudinal MRI study', *Nature Neuroscience*. 2(10): 861–3.

Gladwell, M. (2010). *Blink: The power of thinking, without thinking*. Little, Brown and Company, New York.

Goleman, D. (1996). *Emotional Intelligence: Why it can matter more than IQ.* Simon and Schuster, New York.

Hawton, M. (2013). *Talk Less Listen More: Solutions for children's diffcult behaviour.* Jane Curry Publishing, Sydney.

Hughes, D. (2014). *How to Think Like Sir Alex Ferguson: The business of winning and managing success.* Aurum Press, London.

Lashlie, C. (2010). *He'll Be Okay: Growing gorgeous boys into good men.* HarperCollins Australia, Sydney.

Ledden, E. (2013). *The Presentation Book: How to create it, shape it and deliver it!* Pearson, Sydney.

McKeown, G. (2014). *Essentialism: The disipdined pursuit of less.* Crown Publishing Group, New York.

Patterson, K. et al. (2007). *Influencer: The power to change anything.* McGraw Hill, New York.

Patterson, K. et al. (2013). *Crucial Accountability: Tools for resolving violated expectations, broken comittments and bad behavior.* McGraw Hill, New York.

Peck, M. S. (1978). *The Road Less Travelled: A new psychology of love, traditional values and spiritual growth.* Simon and Schuster, New York.

Phelan, T. (2009). *Surviving Your Adolescents: How to manage and let go of your 13–18-year-olds.* Parent Magic, Chicago.

Seigel, D. (2004). *Parenting From the Inside Out: How a deeper self-understanding can help you raise children who thrive.* Penguin, New York.

Seigel, D. (2014). *Brainstorm: The power and purpose of the teenage brain.* Scribe, Melbourne.

Sutton, R. and Huggy, R. (2014). *Scaling-up Ecellence: Getting to more without settling for less.* Crown Business, New York.

RESOURCES

Below are a few websites that parents may find useful.

Australian Centre for Education in Sleep

www.sleepeducation.net.au

Center for Effective Parenting

A US resource offering information for both parents and professionals.
See www.parenting-ed.org/for-parents/links-for-parents/

Cybersmart

The Cybersmart website provides cybersafety education and awareness for children, young people and parents.
See www.cybersmart.gov.au

DrinkWise Australia

DrinkWise Australia supports young adults and their families to moderate drinking and drinking related behaviours.
See www.drinkwise.org.au

Family Lives UK

A UK organization offering support and various parenting services. See www.familylives.org.uk/advice/teenagers/

Headspace, National Youth Mental Health Foundation

Headspace provides early intervention mental health services to 12- to 25-year-olds and their families.
See www.headspace.org.au

Kiwi Families NZ

Support information for parenting teens.
See www.kiwifamilies.co.nz/topic/teens/

Lifehacker

For instruction how to disable internet access to a smartphone,
see 'Reclaim your life after work by disabling internet access for
smartphones', http://lifehacker.com/5877112/reclaim-your-life-
after-work-by-disabling-internet-access-for-smartphones

The Parenting Place

A New Zealand website offering information and resources.
See www.theparentingplace.com/stage/tweens-and-teens/

Parenting Support Centre

A UK-run website. See www.parenting.co.uk/help/teenagers.
cfm

Parentline

Parentline is a telephone and website service offering support
and guidance to parents. See www.parentline.org.au/ or if in
Australia call 1300 30 1300.

Parents Matter

A Canadian website with a directory for various services.
See www.parentsmatter.ca/index.cfm?fuseaction=page.
viewpage&pageid=618#Middle

Raising Children Network

A government supported parenting website.
See www.raisingchildren.net.au

INDEX

C

can't-let-that-one-go behaviour 56, 57, 75

Caspersen, Dana 97–8

challenges, typical reactions 81–4

change, inability to function 61–2

checklists *see* scripts

circadian screen adjustment app 35

communication *see* conversations

conflict resolution
  PASTA process 75–81
  skills 73–4

consequences
  explaining 87, 184–5
  lacking agreement 175
  legal 184–5
  understanding 186–7

constraints, to enable flexibility 32–6

content, pattern, relationship (CPR) approach *see* CPR (content, pattern, relationship) approach

contrast statements 86, 172

control, over controllables 98–101

controllables 101

conversations
  bottom line 175
  if no progress 158–9
  like football 94–6
  lull in 88–9
  preparation worksheets 168–9, 173–5
  tough ones 97–8
  train wreck approach 111–12
  visualising 99–101

Cooper, Emma
  Agreement (PASTA process) 135–6
  appointment organised 127–8

partying late 110

preparation (PASTA process) 127

reaction to confrontation 124–5

Say (PASTA process) 128–35

train wreck approach 125–6

Cooper, Seb
  Agreement (PASTA process) 154–5
  appointment organised 141–2
  conversation preparation 139–40
  driving lessons 110, 137–55
  reaction to confrontation 137–8
  Say (PASTA process) 142–50
  Tame the Tiger (PASTA process) 150–4
  train wreck approach 138–9

Cooper, Tom
  appointment organised 114–15
  conversation preparation 113–14
  reaction to confrontation 110–11
  Say (PASTA process) 116–19
  Tame the Tiger (PASTA process) 119–22
  train wreck approach 111–12
  violent multi-player video games 109

Cooper family, PASTA process 107–24

CPR (content, pattern, relationship) approach
  In essence 63
  Say (PASTA process)
  stating the problem 79
  tough conversation preparation 173–5
  workplace disputes 60

cross-examination, dealing with 93–4

W